Armies of the Thracians and Dacians
500 BC to AD 150

Armies of the Thracians and Dacians 500 BC to AD 476

History, Organization and Equipment

Gabriele Esposito

Pen & Sword
MILITARY

First published in Great Britain in 2021
by Pen & Sword Military
An imprint of Pen & Sword Books Limited
47 Church Street
Barnsley
South Yorkshire
S70 2AS

Copyright © Gabriele Esposito 2021

ISBN 978 1 52677 274 9

The right of Gabriele Esposito to be identified as
Author of this Work has been asserted by him in accordance
with the Copyright, Designs and Patents Act 1988.

A CIP catalogue record for this book is
available from the British Library

All rights reserved. No part of this book may be reproduced or
transmitted in any form or by any means, electronic or mechanical
including photocopying, recording or by any information storage and
retrieval system, without permission from the Publisher in writing.

Typeset in Adobe Caslon
by Mac Style

Printed and bound in India by Replika Press Pvt. Ltd.

Pen & Sword Books Limited incorporates the imprints of Atlas,
Archaeology, Aviation, Discovery, Family History, Fiction, History, Maritime,
Military, Military Classics, Politics, Select, Transport,
True Crime, Air World, Frontline Publishing, Leo Cooper,
Remember When, Seaforth Publishing, The Praetorian Press, Wharncliffe Local
History, Wharncliffe Transport,
Wharncliffe True Crime and White Owl.

For a complete list of Pen & Sword titles please contact
PEN & SWORD BOOKS LIMITED
47 Church Street, Barnsley, South Yorkshire, S70 2AS, England
E-mail: enquiries@pen-and-sword.co.uk
Website: www.pen-and-sword.co.uk

Contents

Acknowledgements		vii
Introduction		viii
Chapter 1	The Early History of the Thracians	1
Chapter 2	The Thracian expansion and the Odrysian Kingdom	15
Chapter 3	The Thracian 'golden age' and the Rise of Macedonia	37
Chapter 4	Hellenistic Thrace	49
Chapter 5	The Roman Conquest of Thrace	61
Chapter 6	The Early History of the Dacians and the Rise of Burebista	73
Chapter 7	The First War with Rome and the Rise of Decebalus	83
Chapter 8	The Roman Conquest of Dacia	91
Chapter 9	Thracian Military Organization and Tactics	111
Chapter 10	Thracian Military Equipment	125
Chapter 11	Dacian Military Organization and Tactics	151
Chapter 12	Dacian Military Equipment	159
Bibliography		171
The Re-enactors who Contributed to this Book		173
Index		175

Gabriele Esposito is a military historian who works as a freelance author and researcher for some of the most important publishing houses in the military history sector. In particular, he is an expert specializing in uniformology: his interests and expertise range from the ancient civilizations to modern post-colonial conflicts. During recent years he has conducted and published several researches on the military history of the Latin American countries, with special attention on the War of the Triple Alliance and the War of the Pacific. He is among the leading experts on the military history of the Italian Wars of Unification and the Spanish Carlist Wars. His books and essays are published on a regular basis by Osprey Publishing, Winged Hussar Publishing and Libreria Editrice Goriziana; he is also the author of numerous military history articles appearing in specialized magazines like *Ancient Warfare Magazine*, *Medieval Warfare Magazine*, *Classic Arms & Militaria Magazine*, *History of War*, *Guerres et Histoire*, *Focus Storia* and *Focus Storia Wars*.

Acknowledgements

This book is dedicated to my exceptional parents, Maria Rosaria and Benedetto, for the great love and fundamental support that they continue to give me every day. Thanks to their precious observations, derived from long experience, the present work has been much improved. A very special thanks goes to Philip Sidnell, the commissioning editor of my books for Pen & Sword: his love for history and his passion for publishing are essential for the success of our publications. Many thanks also to the production manager of this title, Matt Jones, for his great competence and enthusiasm, and the excellent copyeditor Tony Walton, who as ever played a crucial role. A very special mention goes to the two brilliant re-enactment groups/living history associations that collaborated with their photographs to the creation of this book: without their incredible work of research and re-enactment, the final appearance of this publication would not have been the same. In particular I want to express my deep gratitude to the Bulgarian group 'Ancient Thrace' and the Romanian group 'Historia Renascita', especially to their respective leaders Petar Chapkanov and Catalin Draghici.

Introduction

The main aim of this book is to present a detailed overview of the military history of two important peoples: the Thracians and the Dacians. As we will see, these had a lot in common but were also quite different in many aspects: they inhabited a large portion of Eastern Europe and played an important role in the history of the Ancient World. Both the Thracians and the Dacians were extremely warlike peoples, according to what we know about them from ancient sources and from archaeological researches. They were feared and admired by their enemies, who always had great difficulty in defeating them. The Thracians had lived on the northern edges of the Greek world since the Mycenean period, and thus were well known to the Greeks: they fought against and for the latter on several occasions, contributing in a decisive way to the general development of the Greek art of war. The appearance of the light infantry 'peltast' in the armies of the Greek cities, for example, was mostly the result of the many defeats suffered by the Greeks while fighting against the Thracians. Soldiers from Thrace also made a great contribution to Alexander the Great's victories in Asia: as we will see, they formed a significant part of the Macedonian army that invaded the Persian Empire. During the ensuing Hellenistic period, the Thracians flourished for several decades and served as mercenaries in all the armies of the Mediterranean world. They were admired for their combat skills, and every Hellenistic monarch was ready to pay large sums of money in order to include them in his military forces. Under Lysimachus, one of Alexander the Great's successors, the Thracians were partly 'Hellenized' and their realm was one of the protagonists of the bloody Diadochi Wars. When Rome gradually emerged as the dominant power of the Balkans, the Thracians fought on Macedonia's side and tried to stop the Roman legions. In the end, however, they had to accept the Roman presence on their borders and were progressively transformed into 'vassals' of the Roman Republic. After decades of wars and rebellions, in AD 46 Thrace was organized as a Roman province and the Thracians lost forever their independence. One of their greatest weaknesses had always been that of being politically fragmented, since each Thracian tribe was jealous of its freedom and was constantly at war against the others. Across the centuries, several attempts were made to create a unified 'Thracian Kingdom', especially by the Odrysian tribe, but in the end these did not last for long.

The problems related to political fragmentation were also experienced by the Dacians, who lived in an isolated area of Europe that soon came under the influence of the steppe peoples settled in modern Ukraine. During their early history, the Dacians were dominated for a long time by the Scythians and the Sarmatians; at a certain point, however, a first form of unified 'Dacian Kingdom' emerged, thanks to the efforts of the capable military leader Burebista, who transformed the Dacians into a real regional power and for the first time introduced a 'national spirit' among the various tribes of his people. After Burebista's death, however, the Dacian communities temporarily abandoned their dreams of glory and started to fight against each other, like in the previous centuries. Over time, the traditional isolation of Dacia came to an end and the Roman legions appeared on its frontiers, as a result of which a new phase of political unity began for the Dacians. This led to the ascendancy of Decebalus, one of the greatest military leaders of Antiquity, who fought three wars against the Roman Empire. During the first of these conflicts he was still a simple general, but his great military capabilities allowed him to become the supreme leader of his people. Decebalus modernized Dacia in many ways and created a large 'multi-national' army, following the example of his great predecessor Burebista. As a king, he fought two bloody wars against the Roman Army of Emperor Trajan, who invaded Dacia in order to acquire its great natural resources. The Dacians were strong enough to defeat the Romans on several occasions before their magnificent capital, Sarmizegetusa, was finally conquered by the Empire. Despite the fall of their homeland, some Dacians continued to fight against the Roman Empire until the legions abandoned Dacia around AD 275.

In this book we will analyze all the military campaigns fought by the Thracians and the Dacians, while also describing their military organization with great detail. There will also be sections devoted to the military equipment of these two warrior peoples.

Chapter 1

The Early History of the Thracians

The origins of the Thracians are not very clear from a historical point of view, since their first mention in an ancient written source is present only in Homer's *Iliad*, which was written several centuries after the emergence of the Thracian civilization and thus does not contain any information on the real origins of this people. Archaeology can also tell us very little about the early history of the Thracians, since no permanent settlements or objects have survived from this distant period of history. By analyzing the later culture of the Thracians, however, it has been possible to create a general theory about their origins and their presence in the Balkans. What we know for sure is that the Thracians were an Indo-European people who migrated into Europe more or less around 1500 BC. During that period of the Early Bronze Age, the Indo-Europeans were 'colonizing' most of Europe and were moving from their homeland in the heart of Asia. The newcomers gradually gave birth to new communities in the various European territories, from modern Portugal in the west to Bulgaria in the east. Over time, all the new peoples originating from the Indo-Europeans developed their own cultures and thus became quite different among themselves. All of them, however, retained a fundamental feature of their Indo-European ancestors: they were warlike peoples who considered war as an important component of their daily life. The Indo-Europeans who occupied the Balkans around 1500 BC were divided into two main groups: those of the proto-Illyrians and the proto-Thracians. The former settled in the western half of the Balkans, while the latter colonized the eastern half. Like all the other peoples that were developing from the Indo-Europeans, the proto-Thracians mixed themselves with the indigenous population that had long lived on their newly conquered territories. We don't know if this fusion of different cultures was an easy one, but it was quite rapid: the Indo-European proto-Thracians had a superior civilization compared with the indigenous communities. In particular, they knew how to produce excellent weapons and tools made of bronze, which gave them enormous advantages on the field of battle as well as in agricultural activities. The region inhabited by the proto-Thracians was extremely large, comprising present-day Romania in the north and Bulgaria in the south. The proto-Thracians eventually started to develop two distinct cultures. In the north, due to the strong influence exerted by the steppe peoples living in modern Ukraine,

2   Armies of the Thracians and Dacians, 500 BC to AD 150

Early Thracian warrior from the time of the Trojan War. (*Drawing by Benedetto Esposito*)

Thracian warlord equipped with *rhomphaia* and Chalcidian helmet. (*Photo and copyright by 'Ancient Thrace'*)

the local proto-Thracians partly modified their way of life and thus acquired several new features; in the south, however, the proto-Thracians remained strongly linked to their traditional way of life. As a result of this process, by 1000 BC, the common proto-Thracian culture had disappeared and two new ones had developed: that of the Dacians in the north (modern Romania) and that of the Thracians in the south (Bulgaria). Two new peoples were born, having many characteristics in common but also being quite different among themselves. Consequently, from a historical point of view, we could consider the Thracians as the direct heirs of the proto-Thracian culture and the Dacians as a 'modification' of the latter. The territories of the two peoples were separated by the Danube, which today still marks the border between Romania and Bulgaria. From the early Iron Age, the Thracians started to have their own history, the early phase of which we know very little about. What we know for sure, however, is that by 1200–1100 BC (the period during which the *Iliad* was composed), the Thracians consisted of several different tribes who interacted with the Mycenean Civilization of Greece. In the Homeric poem, we find the Thracians as allies of the Trojans in their long war against the Myceneans (called 'Greeks' in the *Iliad*). In particular, the Thracians are described as being organized into three distinct groups: a first group, having as war leaders Acamas and Peirous, came from the Dardanelles area (at that time known as the Hellespont); a second group, that of the Cicones, had Euphemus as leader and came from southern Thrace; a third, having the famous King Rhesus as its main leader, came from northern Thrace. All these Thracian communities were long-time allies of the Trojans.

This was probably due to the fact that Troy exerted a strong influence over the Hellespont, because of the great commercial importance of the Dardanelles Straits. Indeed, the local Thracians could have been under a sort of Trojan 'protectorate' because control of their land was vital for the nearby city described in the *Iliad*. The strategic location of Troy, on the western coast of Anatolia, had allowed its enterprising inhabitants to create a flourishing trading empire, which controlled all the major commercial routes of the eastern Aegean and, more in general, of the eastern Mediterranean. The city was built just a few miles from the Dardanelles Straits and controlled the Bosphorus, through which every day passed loads of goods coming from the Black Sea and going into the Aegean. Troy was also the terminal of the so-called 'way of bronze and copper', a commercial route across which the two most important metals of the Late Bronze Age were transported from Central Europe to Anatolia. This route used the Danube as a waterway and was fundamental for the economy of the Black Sea area. Troy sold bronze and copper in all the great markets of the Ancient Middle East, in an age during which the latter was dominated by the powerful Hittite Empire. The Trojans imposed taxes on all the ships transporting goods that passed through the Dardanelles, and thus tax revenues were the main income of Troy together with the large sums earned from the commerce of metals. However, despite being enormously rich, the city was not fully independent: the Hittites had some sort of control over it. By 1300 BC, they already ruled central and eastern Anatolia in a direct way, and it was in the former region that they had their imperial capital of Hattusas (not far from modern Ankara). The western part of Anatolia was organized in a semi-independent confederation of minor states that was guided by the city of Troy. This was known as the Confederation of Assuwa and comprised twenty-two states of different dimensions. The confederation was placed under the military protection of the Hittites from its foundation and was constantly menaced by the expansionism of the Myceneans coming from Greece. These Myceneans wished to conquer the western coast of Anatolia in order to expand their commercial routes and assume control over the terminus of the 'way of bronze and copper'. To do this, however, they would have been obliged to fight a war not only against the military forces of the Confederation of Assuwa, but also

Thracian warlord wearing a Chalcidian helmet imported from Greece. (*Photo and copyright by 'Ancient Thrace'*)

against the vast Hittite Army. The diplomatic relations between the confederation guided by Troy and the Hittites, however, were not always positive: in the Hittite documents, for example, we find mention of a large revolt taking place in western Anatolia against the local Hittite garrisons. This was crushed by the Hittite Army, but surely had some important political consequences. Around 1200–1100 BC, the Myceneans finally decided that the time had come to invade the Confederation of Assuwa. We don't know if they took this initiative because the Hittites were involved in a war against Egypt on the southern borders of their empire; we know for sure, however, that the Confederation of Assuwa was not supported by the Hittite Army during the war that has been described in the *Iliad*. The Trojans, being at the head of a confederation that acted as a sort of 'buffer zone' between two great empires, had developed an effective military structure, the strongest point of which was the contingents sent by the allied communities. Some decades before the outbreak of the hostilities, another similar conflict had already been fought on the territory of western Anatolia. We know this from an ancient Hittite document, known as the 'Tawagalawa Letter'. This was written by a Hittite king and directed to the supreme leader of the Myceneans (who were known as 'Ahhiyawa' by the Hittites). In the letter, the Hittite monarch cites a war that had recently been fought between his empire and the Myceneans for possession of Troy (which was called 'Wilusa' by the Hittites). This specific passage in the document confirms the fact that the Myceneans were interested in the conquest of Troy and that a war (albeit brief) had already been fought between them and the Hittites for its possession. Another Hittite document, produced a few years before the outbreak of the conflict described in the *Iliad*, adds some more details to this historical reconstruction. This, known as the 'Alaksandu Treaty', was sent by the Hittite King Muwatalli II to a new King of Troy named Alaksandu. In the text of the treaty, the Hittite monarch recalls the ancient alliance existing between his empire and the city of Wilusa, and expresses his hope that this could continue for another three centuries. This information seems to confirm that the Confederation of Assuwa had a long history.

Our main source of information on the contingents of allies that fought on Troy's side against the Myceneans is the so-called 'Trojan Catalogue', a long list of military detachments that is present in Book 2 of the *Iliad*. This reports all the troops mobilized by the Confederation of Assuwa, with the names of their commanders and the geographical area from which they came. The 'Trojan Catalogue' lists sixteen contingents sent from twelve different peoples/communities, which were under the command of twenty-six major war leaders and lived in thirty-three different zones of the Trojan Empire. The first detachments to be listed are those from Troy and its surroundings; the population inhabiting the city had also built several minor

Thracian peltast with full personal equipment. (*Photo and copyright by 'Ancient Thrace'*)

Thracian peltast with *zeira* cloak. (*Photo and copyright by 'Ancient Thrace'*)

settlements in the Dardanelles area, and thus was not concentrated only in the capital. The inhabitants of Troy and its surroundings were collectively known as Dardanians, a name from which the term 'Dardanelles' derives. In total, in addition to the 'proper' Trojans, there were four semi-independent communities of Dardanians living in the countryside of north-western Anatolia. The remaining eleven allied contingents were provided by independent tribes/peoples that were all part of the Confederation of Assuwa: Pelasgians, Thracians, Cicones, Paeonians, Paphlagonians, Halizones, Mysians, Phrygians, Maeonians, Carians and Lycians. As anticipated above, two of the eleven peoples/communities were Thracian: the Thracians from the Dardanelles area (who were the only ones to be called 'Thracians' by the Trojans) and the Cicones (who were known by the peculiar name of their tribe). The Cicones lived along the southern coast of Thrace and were among the most loyal allies of Troy, to the point that after the city's fall, the Myceneans launched a punitive expedition against them (with the main objective of raiding their rich settlements). We don't know why the Thracians of the Dardanelles were listed as a separate group; probably they had migrated only recently into that region and did not come from southern Thrace like the Cicones.

Of the allied contingents listed in the 'Trojan Catalogue', another two also had very strong links with the Thracian tribes: these were the Paeonians and the Phrygians. We know very little of the Paeonians, but judging from the few words of their language that have survived in ancient sources, they were a tribe living in the heart of the Balkans. They were of mixed Illyrian and Thracian stock and their home territory was located between the regions occupied by the Illyrians and those inhabited by the Thracians. They had many characteristics in common with the Thracian tribes, but could not be considered as part of the Thracian culture because their community had emerged from the fusion of two different Indo-European peoples. The Phrygians, however, are difficult to consider as a distinct people from the Thracians: they were, in fact, the 'Thracians of Asia'. Shortly before the outbreak of the Trojan War, the Thracian tribe of the Bryges had moved into Anatolia from Thrace, having probably been invited to do so by the Trojans, who wanted to count on them as loyal allies in Anatolia. After moving into modern Turkey, the Bryges assumed the new denomination of Phrygians and organized their own state in Asia. Over time, especially from 1100–1000 BC, they started to be increasingly influenced by the local cultures of Anatolia. However, they never lost their Thracian identity despite being considered as a 'new' people by all the Anatolian communities living around them and by the 'Thracians of Europe'. Due to their strong cultural links with the other Thracian tribes, the Phrygians will be analyzed in this book as part of the Thracians; the same will be the casew with the Paeonians, whose history was quite different from that of the other tribes living in the Balkans.

Thracian peltast equipped with *pelte* shield and light javelins. (*Photo and copyright by 'Ancient Thrace'*)

The Thracians of the Dardanelles, Cicones, Paeonians and Phrygians made up the most numerous component of the army deployed by the Confederation of Assuwa; they all spoke the same language and fought in the same way, but their war leaders were able to communicate with the Trojan commanders by using the Luwian language (at that time the *lingua franca* of western Anatolia). During the last phase of the Trojan War, another group of Thracians came to Anatolia in order

Thracian tribal warriors; the one on the left carries a *kopis* sword while that on the right has a knife with a curved blade. (*Photo and copyright by 'Ancient Thrace'*)

to support the Confederation of Assuwa. This was led by Rhesus and came from the northern part of Thrace. This region was not part of the Trojan sphere of influence in the Dardanelles, which explains why the warriors of Rhesus are not listed in the 'Trojan Catalogue'. More than semi-subjects, in fact, these northern Thracians were independent allies.

The arrival of Rhesus' men in the theatre of operations, according to the *Iliad*, made a great impression on the Myceneans. According to the description contained in the poem, the leaders of this Thracian contingent wore golden armour of excellent quality and used superb war chariots to move on the battlefield. Apparently, they seemed invincible and their sudden arrival could have changed the outcome of the war. The Myceneans, however, attacked the Thracians before they could reach Troy and join their allies. According to the *Iliad*, Rhesus and his warriors were massacred during a night attack, eliminated as a potential menace before their military potential could be deployed.

The passage of the poem that describes the Thracian military forces is particularly interesting, since it provides two important elements: first, the tribes of northern Thrace were already rich enough to equip their most prominent warriors with full armour; second, the Thracians were already famous as horse breeders by the time of the Trojan War. According to our primary source, the Thracian horses were the best in the world, being greatly valued by the Myceneans. The Thracians are also mentioned in the *Odyssey*, in which there is a description of an attack launched by Odysseus against the Cicones of southern Thrace. The Myceneans, returning to their homeland after having destroyed Troy, decided to launch a retaliatory raid against the Thracians who had supported the Confederation of Assuwa with their troops. Initially, the Mycenean raid had success, the main settlement of the Cicones (Ismara) being conquered and pillaged. At a certain point, however, major reinforcements from the other settlements of the tribe attacked Odysseus and his men. After suffering severe losses, the Myceneans were forced to leave Ismara and went back to their ships.

Shortly after the fall of Troy, the world in which the Thracians had lived until that moment changed forever as the Bronze Age came to an abrupt end after a series of incredible events took place in south-eastern Europe and the Middle East. Natural disasters and mass migrations changed the face of the civilized world forever, causing the beginning of a new historical era known as the Iron Age. This started with the collapse of two civilizations, those of the Hittites and the Myceneans. The Myceneans came under attack from a large confederation of warlike communities, commonly known as the 'Sea Peoples'. These invaded mainland Greece and also settled on the Middle East's coastline; even Egypt ran the risk of being invaded by these foreigners, who were defeated by the pharaohs only with great difficulty. We know very little of

Thracian warrior armed with spear. (*Photo and copyright by 'Ancient Thrace'*)

the Sea Peoples, but apparently they comprised several communities who came from different areas of the eastern Mediterranean. Their mass migrations caused the fall of the Mycenean kingdoms in Greece and led to the beginning of the Greek Dark Ages, while in Asia, the invasions and raids of the Sea Peoples were among the main causes of the dissolution of the Hittite Empire. Luckily for them, the Thracians were not affected in any significant way by the incredible events that took place in the last years of the Bronze Age. Their home territories were never attacked on a large scale by the Sea Peoples, and thus they did not suffer serious human losses. After the political assets of south-eastern Europe and the Middle East stabilized, the Thracians understood that they could benefit greatly from the disappearance of the ancient empires located on their borders. In the west, they could now expand towards northern Greece; in the east, the Phrygians could consolidate their presence in Anatolia. By 800 BC, the 'Thracians of Asia' had organized their territorial possessions in present-day Turkey as a unified kingdom, having as its capital the city of Gordium. Thanks to the power vacuum caused by the fall of the Hittite Empire, the Phrygians could expand their realm by conquering new territories in the heart of Anatolia (where the ancient Hittite capital of Hattusas had been located). It was during this period that another two Thracian tribes, the Bithyni and the Thyni, arrived in present-day northern Turkey and established a new kingdom similar to Phrygia. This became known as Bithynia, from the name of the two communities that created it, and was located north-east of the Phrygian lands. In order to settle in Anatolia, the Bithyni and the Thyni had to defeat the local population of the Mysians, who had been part of the Confederation of Assuwa and apparently suffered greatly from the collapse of the Hittite Empire.

Chapter 2

The Thracian expansion and the Odrysian Kingdom

At the beginning of the eighth century BC, the Thracians could already be considered as one of the most flourishing peoples of Europe: they occupied a vast Balkan area located south of the Danube and had established firm control over a significant part of Anatolia. Both Phrygia and Bithynia eventually became proper 'Asian' kingdoms, but their populations never lost their original Thracian culture. As we will see, both these Thracian states of Anatolia would play an important role in the political and military history of ancient Turkey. The Thracians of Europe, on the other hand, developed no form of unified kingdom for a long time. They were divided into over forty tribes, which were constantly at war against each other: Thracian society was an extremely warlike one, in which warfare was considered one of the most important elements in a man's ordinary life. From an economic point of view, the Thracians practised breeding much more than agriculture: the great majority of them, in fact, were shepherds and lived thanks to the products obtained from their sheep/goats. Inter-tribal skirmishes and raids were usually sparked by disagreements among shepherds about control of the pastures. The majority of the Thracians did not live in permanent settlements, following their herds during most of the year. As a result, until the arrival of the first Greek colonists, Thrace did not have any major city. Raiding the village of a rival tribe was normal practice for a semi-nomad Thracian community, since skirmishes and small 'local' wars were a great occasion to enlarge herds by capturing sheep/goats from the enemy. The territory of Thrace, mostly covered by hills, was not well suited to armies equipped with heavy armour and moving in close formations. The only way to move rapidly and fight effectively in the Thracian motherland was to act as skirmishers, equipped with throwing weapons and trained in light infantry tactics. The territory of present-day Bulgaria, however, also comprises some plains, where the Thracians could breed horses and where some excellent cavalry contingents could be raised. The Thracian tribes were distinguished between 'mountain' and 'plain' ones, according to the morphology of the hills or valleys on which they lived.

According to ancient authors such as Herodotus, the Thracians were the most numerous people of Europe: if united into a single kingdom, they could have defeated and conquered all the ancient nations living along their borders. Luckily for

Thracian warrior armed with javelin. (*Photo and copyright by 'Ancient Thrace'*)

Thracian peltast with full personal equipment. (*Photo and copyright by 'Ancient Thrace'*)

the latter, however, the Thracians always preferred inter-tribal warfare to invasions directed against foreign peoples. Potentially, thanks to their great military capabilities, they could have been one of the leading powers of Antiquity. By the end of the Greek Dark Ages, around 650 BC, the Thracians were already famous throughout the Mediterranean world for their combat skills and unrivalled courage on the battlefield. Consequently, they started to be employed on a large scale as mercenaries by several ancient kingdoms. In Thrace, the profession of warrior was highly honoured and considered as superior to all others. Showing courage in battle was fundamental for a Thracian man to acquire a solid personal reputation. Generally speaking, however, Thracian warriors were not famous for their martial discipline: they loved plunder more than anything else, and this frequently caused them serious problems during a battle or campaign. On many occasions, as we will see, the Thracians did not respect orders when an enemy camp was conquered or an enemy city was occupied: they had to pillage every enemy location they crossed, even if doing so prevented them from pursuing and crushing an enemy that had already been defeated. The Thracians obeyed only strong war leaders, who came from their own tribes: it was particularly difficult for foreign commanders, in fact, to secure their loyalty. When serving as mercenaries, if not paid properly and on time, they were prone to mutinies and revolts. It was not uncommon for Thracians to join the enemy, if the latter's leader offered them large amounts of gold or a good opportunity to plunder a rich city. The Thracians never lost their original character of semi-nomadic raiders, even after centuries of close contact with the major civilizations of the Mediterranean. Nothing was more important for them than personal wealth, and every possible method to augment this was considered as legitimate.

Much of what we know about the Thracians comes from Greek and Roman sources, since they have not left any written material themselves. For this reason, we know very little of their early history and have only a very scanty idea of the alphabet they used. Despite this, we can take for granted that they had no problems in using violence against their enemies: while plundering a territory or if well paid as mercenaries, they had no hesitation in carrying out mass executions or massacres. Well known for their cruelty, they were also famous for being high-spirited: singing and dancing were two fundamental components of their daily life, together with drinking wine in enormous quantities. It should be pointed out, however, that their way of life was not so different from that of many other ancient peoples, and that their technological skills were by no means rudimentary. They were able to produce deadly weapons with metals, as well as working tools. Although the Thracians were not used to living in urban centres or practising commerce on a large scale, their simple economy was solid enough to create frequent demographic booms. The

Thracian tribal warrior wearing a fur over his shoulders. (*Photo and copyright by 'Ancient Thrace'*)

Thracian peltast wearing *zeira* cloak. (*Photo and copyright by 'Ancient Thrace'*)

Duel between two Thracian warriors. (*Photo and copyright by 'Ancient Thrace'*)

history of the Thracians, however, changed dramatically when they came in contact with the first Greek colonists moving to the Thracian coastline. With the end of the so-called Dark Ages, the population of mainland Greece started to grow at an impressive rate, and all the newly founded *poleis* (independent cities/states) had to introduce some measures to control the demographics of their communities. Greece was still a poor country at that time, its territory mostly covered with mountains. Consequently, the Greek cities could not practise agriculture on a large scale and were forced to resettle a considerable number of their citizens outside the borders of mainland Greece. During the eighth and seventh centuries BC, many thousands of Greek colonists departed from their mother cities, going in search of new lands to found their own *poleis*. These great migratory movements of the Greeks were directed towards the western Mediterranean, where they created many flourishing colonies in southern Italy, but also towards the coastline of the Black Sea area. The latter extended from Thrace in the west to the Caucasus in the east, crossing a large portion of modern Ukraine in the north.

The coastline of Thrace, extending from the Chalcidian Peninsula to the delta of the Danube, was the first target of the Greek colonists during their eastward expansion. When it was found that the hills inhabited by the Thracians were rich in precious metals like gold or silver, the Greek penetration in Thrace became significant. The *poleis* of mainland Greece were constantly searching for new natural resources in order to sustain the great commercial expansion of their communities: by founding new colonies in the east, they could resolve their problems of over-population and also acquire control over strategic natural resources in foreign lands. To build new settlements, however, the Greeks were forced to fight with the local Thracian tribes, who had no intention of welcoming the foreigners. Indeed, during their early attempts to colonize the Thracian coastline, the Greeks experienced many difficulties. The local population was a warlike one and the whole region was still in a 'wild' state, according to Greek standards of the time. Thrace, however, was a land of opportunities, and the Greeks did not give up their colonization drive. During this early period, which lasted until the outbreak of the Persian Wars in the fifth century BC, the Greeks founded several new settlements along the coastline of southern Thrace. In particular, they penetrated into the strategic Chersonese Peninsula, which while part of Europe from a geographical point of view, makes up the western side of the Dardanelles Straits. For this reason, the Greeks sought control over this peninsula, which was also known as the 'Thracian Chersonese'. The rich commercial outposts established by the Greeks on the southern coast of Thrace soon transformed themselves into proper cities, whose relations with the Thracians were quite complicated. After decades of minor wars and frequent skirmishes, it became clear to the Thracian tribes that the Greek colonies could not be destroyed by them. The colonies were well defended by thick walls, and the Thracians were unable to conduct proper siege operations. During the following centuries, these centres would play an important historical role by connecting the Greek culture with that of the Thracians.

The sixth century BC was an age of great turmoil for the Ancient Middle East, since it saw the emergence of the great Persian Empire that was ruled by the Achaemenid Dynasty founded by Cyrus the Great. The Persians, originally a nomadic population living in the vast territories of present-day Iran, gradually conquered all the regions that had formerly been part of the Assyrian Empire, and later occupied Babylon after a protracted siege. After obtaining complete dominance over Mesopotamia, they turned their attention to Anatolia and the rich kingdoms that were located in the western part of Asia. Among these were Phrygia and Bithynia. Phrygia had been a significant local power in Anatolia during the previous two centuries, especially between 720 and 700 BC, when it was able to establish good diplomatic relations with the Assyrian Empire. In 695 BC, however, the Kingdom of Phrygia was invaded by the Cimmerians, who destroyed its flourishing capital of Gordium. The Cimmerians were a nomadic people living in the steppes of Ukraine and southern Russia; they had much in common with the Scythians, but their culture was rather different. Around 715 BC, the Cimmerians started to invade the Middle East by moving from

Thracian warrior equipped with kopis sword and pelte shield. (Photo and copyright by 'Ancient Thrace')

their home territories in the Caucasus. However, after having been repulsed by the Assyrians, they turned west and attacked Anatolia. After plundering Phrygia, they continued to have a strong presence in the eastern part of present-day Turkey. The smaller states of Anatolia were greatly damaged by the Cimmerian raids and were soon conquered by the Kingdom of Lydia, which absorbed several of them to emerge as a significant regional power. The Lydians conducted many campaigns against the Cimmerians, with the objective of expelling them from the lands located south of the Caucasus. After decades of violence and clashes, by 620 BC the northern invaders had been expelled from Anatolia. As a result, the entire territory of Phrygia became part of the Kingdom of Lydia (whose rich capital was the city of Sardes). The Phrygians had definitively lost their independence, and now their homeland was located on the border between two expanding states: the Lydians in the west and the Persians in the east.

After the Cimmerians abandoned the Middle East, a new political order emerged in the region. The Assyrian Empire disappeared and for a short time the ancient city of Babylon assumed control over most of Mesopotamia. Meanwhile, in Iran, the Persians emerged as a strong military power and started to expand their territories towards modern Iraq. At a certain point, they turned their attention towards the flourishing Kingdom of Lydia. The latter was ruled by the famous King Croesus, who feared (correctly) that his realm was the next target of the Persian armies. He did not wait for the Persian invasion, but instead decided to attack first in 547 BC; at that time he was allied with Sparta, the Neo-Babylonian Empire and Egypt, so victory against the expanding Persians seemed possible. After some inconclusive clashes fought in central Anatolia, the decisive battle took place in 546 BC at Thymbra. Croesus was soundly defeated and had to retreat to his capital of Sardes, which was soon besieged and then conquered by the advancing Persians. The defeated king was captured and his realm was absorbed into the Persian Empire. A few years later, in 539 BC, Cyrus the Great would also occupy Babylon and thus complete the military conquest of the Middle East. Phrygia, like the rest of the Kingdom of Lydia, became part of the Persian Empire and was organized as a satrapy with a Persian governor. The Kingdom of Bithynia had the same destiny as Phrygia: invaded and raided by the Cimmerians, it was absorbed into the Kingdom of Lydia and later annexed by the Persians after the defeat of Croesus. When the satrapy of Phrygia was established, Bithynia was made part of it. The Achaemenids thus unified the Thracians of Asia into a single administrative entity, which provided large numbers of excellent soldiers for the Persian Army. According to ancient sources, the Phrygians were an important component of the Persian expeditionary forces that conquered the Greek cities on the western coast of Anatolia. The latter had lived in peace during the age of Croesus,

Thracian warrior armed with *kopis* sword. (*Photo and copyright by 'Ancient Thrace'*)

Thracian warrior carrying a deadly *rhomphaia*. (*Photo and copyright by 'Ancient Thrace'*)

enjoying great political autonomy, albeit being part (at least formally) of the Kingdom of Lydia. Cyrus the Great soon organized an expedition against the Greek cities of Asia Minor, led by his Median general Harpagus, who was able to subdue the *poleis* of western Anatolia after a brief campaign. However, the Greeks had no intention of giving up the fight.

The Greek *poleis* proved very difficult to rule for the Persians, refusing to pay taxes and always being ready to rise up in open revolt. In most areas of his growing empire, like in Lydia, Cyrus the Great had always formed alliances with the various local aristocracies after defeating them. Such a political operation, however, proved impossible with the Greek cities of Asia Minor, where all citizens had more or less the same rights and social position. For the first time, the Persians were dealing with a people made up of free individuals and not of subjects used to serving under a supreme monarch. The Achaemenids sponsored the ascendancy of tyrants in several *poleis*, but this was not enough to secure their control over Asia Minor. Most of their allied tyrants were soon killed or expelled by popular revolts of their citizens. The majority of the Greeks from Asia were sure that their mainland 'brothers' would have helped them against the foreign invaders, since by the beginning of the fifth century BC, western Anatolia was widely considered to be part of the Greek world. The Persians were well aware of this, but had plans to continue their expansion towards Greece in the future. Consequently, they tried to form a network of alliances with various cities of mainland Greece in view of the future developments. In 513 BC, new Persian monarch Darius I conducted a first campaign in Scythia and Thrace, with the objective of conquering areas of Europe before starting to organize a larger invasion of the southern Balkans. The Scythians, a strong nomadic people living in present-day Ukraine, had been allies of the Persians during the campaigns fought by the latter against Babylon, but had then turned into a dangerous menace for the vast empire that the Achaemenids were building. As a result, hostilities broke out between the Persians and Scythians. Darius, wishing to eliminate once and for all these nomads, mounted an assault against their main European territories of southern Ukraine after crossing the Bosphorus from Asia Minor using a bridge of boats.

While moving north, the Persians crossed Thrace and subdued (albeit temporarily) most of the local tribes. The Scythians used scorched earth tactics throughout the campaign and were thereby able to retreat across the immense plains of Ukraine without fighting a single pitched battle against the Persians. In the end the expedition organized by Darius proved inconclusive and ended with the retreat of the Achaemenids to their own territories. Thrace, however, remained under Persian control and was formally organized as a satrapy known as Skudra. The local tribes, however, resented foreign rule from the outset and were ready to revolt against the

28 Armies of the Thracians and Dacians, 500 BC to AD 150

Thracian warrior armed with two-handed *rhomphaia*. (*Photo and copyright by 'Ancient Thrace'*)

Thracian tribal warrior equipped with a knife with a curved blade and small oval shield. (*Photo and copyright by 'Ancient Thrace'*)

Persians at the first opportunity. In 492 BC, a new Persian expeditionary corps, guided by Mardonius (son-in-law of Darius I), departed from the Anatolia region of Cilicia with the objective of crushing the continuing Thracian rebellions. The Persian Army advanced by land up to the Hellespont in northern Anatolia, marching along the coastline in order to retain direct contact with the Achaemenid fleet. At this point, all the troops were embarked on the ships and then crossed the Hellespont without particular problems. Once in Europe, the Persians focused on re-subjugating the Thracian tribes one by one: since the latter were politically divided, the reoccupation of southern Thrace was not a difficult task for Mardonius. By now the Persians had a solid base in Europe. At this point, instead of moving north to once more fight against the Scythians, the Achaemenid army moved west in order to enter Greece from the north. In 490 BC, the Persians attacked Greece for the first time with a relatively small expeditionary force of just 25,000 soldiers. This First Persian War ended with Greek victory at the Battle of Marathon, during which 9,000 Athenian hoplites and 1,000 of their allies from Plataea were able to repulse the invaders without suffering significant losses. In 480 BC, however, new Persian monarch Xerxes organized a massive invasion of mainland Greece and assembled a large army made up of contingents from each corner of the Achaemenid Empire. The Second Persian War was not just a punitive expedition like the conflict of 490 BC, but a proper expansionist campaign that involved the best elements of the Persian Army. According to Herodotus, the Thracians of Europe and the Phrygians of Asia made a significant military contribution to the Persian expedition of 480 BC, providing Xerxes with large and excellent contingents. These took part in all the major military events of the conflict, which ended with two resounding defeats for the Persians.

Thrace was, together with Macedonia, the main base of the Persian Army during the operations of 480–479 BC. After the Achaemenid troops were defeated by the Greeks at Plataea, however, the Persian positions in Europe became unstable. The Thracians thereby saw an opportunity to free themselves from foreign rule by exploiting the temporary weakness of the Persians. They revolted against their Achaemenid commanders and attacked what remained of the Persian military forces, which had been obliged by the Greeks to retreat across Thrace. By using their usual guerrilla hit-and-run tactics, the Thracians caused significant losses to their former overlords and expelled them from Europe. Thrace was again independent, after more than thirty years of Persian rule. Although the Persians had not been particularly strict, the Thracians had never accepted the presence of foreign forces in their territory, as well as the possibility that a distant king could ask them to raise military units for his own campaigns. During the brief existence of the Skudra satrapy, however, the Thracians had experienced some form of unification, which proved positive for

Thracian slinger. (*Photo and copyright by 'Ancient Thrace'*)

32 Armies of the Thracians and Dacians, 500 BC to AD 150

Thracian slinger, using his deadly weapon. (*Photo and copyright by 'Ancient Thrace'*)

their development. The events of the Persian Wars, in fact, had shown them the importance of being united to counter foreign aggression. However, with the defeat of the Persians, the Greeks represented a new menace for Thrace. Guided by Athens, the Greeks were now entering into a phase of commercial expansionism and were in search of new natural resources to support their growing economy. Around 470 BC, to fill the power vacuum left by the Persians and to prevent Greek expansionism, a first independent and unified kingdom started to emerge in Thrace. This was created by a very capable leader named Teres, who was at the head of one of the most important Thracian tribes, the Odrysians. These tribesmen, who lived in the fertile plain of the Hebrus River and were extremely numerous, were famous for their combat capabilities and had always been one of the leading Thracian tribes. Under the guidance of Teres, they were able to impose their will on most of the communities living in present-day Bulgaria and unified the region as the Odrysian Kingdom.

Under Sitalces, the successor of Teres, the new state reached its greatest territorial extent: in the north, its border with the Scythian territories was marked by the Danube, while in the east, it extended towards Macedonia up to the Strymon River. On the

Thracian warrior armed with a sling. (*Photo and copyright by 'Ancient Thrace'*)

eastern and southern coastline, however, it did not exert any form of control over the various colonies that the Greeks had already established in Thrace. Around 430 BC, these comprised the following commercial centres: Abdera, Aenos, Lysimachia and Byzantium on the southern coastline; and Apollonia Pontike, Archialos, Messembria, Odessos, Byzone, Tomoi and Istros on the eastern coastline. Byzantium, in particular, was the most flourishing of these cities since it controlled the Bosphorus Straits that connected the Black Sea with the Aegean. After Sitalces' death, the Odrysian Kingdom experienced serious internal difficulties. Many of the tribes started to revolt against the Odrysians, heralding a new age of political fragmentation. The unified state had never had a centralized organization, and its existence had always been based on the military supremacy of the Odrysians. Although the Odrysians had exerted control over most of Thrace for a period, for some areas of the country this was only nominal. The majority of the Thracian tribes did not want to live in a centralized state, since they considered the other communities of their own people as traditional enemies. The brief experience of the Odrysian Kingdom was not able to cancel the endemic inter-tribal rivalries that had always damaged the social development of the Thracians. During Sitalces' reign, the Thracians had been a great military power in the

Thracian tribal warrior blowing his horn. (*Photo and copyright by 'Ancient Thrace'*)

Balkans: in the north, they had stopped Scythian expansionism on the Danube (after the mounted warriors of the steppes had already occupied Dacia); in the south-west, they formed military alliances with the Greeks and participated in the long-running Peloponnesian War. Sitalces, also known as Sitalces the Great because of his many victories, decided to side with Athens during the latter conflict, fighting against the Spartans and their allies. In 429 BC, the Odrysian Kingdom assembled a large army of over 150,000 warriors and invaded Macedonia, which was an ally of Sparta during the Peloponnesian War. The Thracians were able to conquer Macedonia after a brief campaign, and later moved south in order to attack the Greek cities that were located in the Chalcidian Peninsula and that supported Sparta.

According to the plans that had been agreed with the Athenians, Sitalces' large army would have been supported by the Athenian navy during the difficult siege operations against the Chalcidian cities. When the Thracians arrived in the Chalcidian Peninsula, however, they found no Athenians to support their efforts. Apparently, the Athenians had been greatly impressed by the rapid invasion of Macedonia and thus now considered the Thracians as a potential menace: an army of 150,000 'barbarian' warriors who could have easily occupied most of Greece after conquering the Chalcidian cities. After pillaging the Chalcidian Peninsula for several days and being unable to invest the Greek cities without the Athenian siege engines, the Thracians went back to their homeland after having taken enormous amounts of gold. In 424 BC, Sitalces the Great died while fighting an internal war against the tribe of the Triballi (who had never been part of unified Thrace). His realm was then divided into several smaller kingdoms, ruled by different members of the Odrysian royal family. We can only imagine what could have happened if the Thracians would have remained part of a single state, which had more or less the same revenues as Athens and which could count on massive military forces. The sudden collapse of the Odrysian Kingdom favoured the rapid resurgence of Macedonia in the heart of the Balkans and led to an increase in Greek influence over Thrace. As mentioned above, the Triballi had never been part of the Odrysian Kingdom: they were considered as the most barbarian of all Thracians by the Greeks and were settled on the north-western border of Thrace. Here they lived in a state of constant war against the Schytians, who had invaded Dacia and who frequently launched rapid incursions south of the Danube. On the western border of their homeland, the Triballi were often at war with the nearby Illyrian communities. Consequently, most of their life was spent fighting against other warlike peoples. Over time they acquired several cultural features of their enemies and thus started to be considered as different from the usual Thracians. However, their traditional culture was never modified to the point of becoming a new one.

Thracian warrior carrying a standard. (*Photo and copyright by 'Ancient Thrace'*)

Chapter 3

The Thracian 'golden age' and the Rise of Macedonia

During Sitalces' reign, Thracian culture had already started to be increasingly influenced by Greek civilization. Greek language became the *lingua franca* of the Odrysian Kingdom and started to be spoken by the members of Sitalces' court. In addition, the Greek alphabet was introduced in order to create a form of Thracian script that was to be used for administrative purposes. After the fall of the Odrysian Kingdom, the Thracians continued to play an important part in the military events of the Peloponnesian War. In 423 BC, the Athenians attacked the Chalcidian cities of Mende and Scione with an army that comprised around 1,000 Thracian mercenaries/allies, then in the following year, a large contingent of Thracians was included in the Spartan expeditionary force that defeated the Chalcidian city of Amphipolis (which was allied to Athens). Both Sparta and Athens employed large numbers of Thracian warriors during the military operations conducted in the Chalcidian Peninsula, which was rich in important natural resources and whose cities included allies of Athens and supporters of Sparta. The Chalcidian theatre of operations was quite far from both Athens and Sparta, and was difficult to reach by land or by sea. Instead of sending large expeditionary corps to this isolated area, the two powers fighting in the Peloponnesian War preferred raising local forces of Thracian allies and mercenaries. In 413 BC, the Athenians contracted 1,300 Thracian mercenaries to take part in their ill-fated expedition against the Sicilian allies of Sparta. When these arrived in Athens, however, the naval expedition organized by Alcibiades had already set sail for Sicily. The Athenians ordered the Thracians to march back home, but also to attack two cities in Boeotia that were allies of Sparta during their return. The Thracians carried out their task with the usual violence, killing every inhabitant of one of these two *poleis*, Mycalessos. The Thebans sent their strong cavalry forces to intercept the retreating Thracians, but the Thracians were able to repulse the attacks of the horsemen and returned home without further problems.

Around 407 BC, what had been the Odrysian Kingdom now consisted of two independent states. The Athenians put great efforts into concluding a military alliance with both, and were finally able to employ large numbers of Thracian warriors against the Spartans. The Athenian leader Alcibiades had understood very well the military potential of the Thracians and, thanks to his personal charisma, had established a

Thracian warrior with a standard. (*Photo and copyright by 'Ancient Thrace'*)

Thracian warriors with *labrys* double-headed axe (left) and standard (right). (*Photo and copyright by 'Ancient Thrace'*)

good relationship with their most prominent chiefs. He used the Thracian warriors to attack Sparta's allies in the Hellespont region, obtaining significant results: several Greek cities in the area that opposed Athens were destroyed by the Thracians or obliged to pay them a regular tribute. Alcibiades did his best to reinforce the authority of the two Thracian kings who had formed an alliance with Athens, for example by attacking and plundering the lands of those few Thracian tribes that were still independent from the two main realms. In 401 BC, a major civil war erupted inside the Persian Empire between legitimate monarch Artaxerxes II and the rebellious satrap Cyrus the Younger. Cyrus could not count on large numbers of Persian soldiers, and consequently was forced to recruit many Greek and Thracian mercenaries in order to fight against Artaxerxes. This Persian civil war witnessed the participation of the famous 'Ten Thousand', commanded by Xenophon, who were all Greek mercenary soldiers hired by Cyrus. Attached to the 10,000 Greeks there were also 900 Thracians, who fought with them at the decisive Battle of Cunaxa. This encounter saw the defeat of Cyrus the Younger and obliged the 'Ten Thousand' Greeks to march back home. The retreat of Xenophon's men was extremely long and difficult; they were pursued by the victorious Persian forces and had to cross many hostile lands. Although some Thracians abandoned the 'Ten Thousand' during the retreat, most of them remained loyal to Xenophon. After many minor battles and an exhausting march, the Greek and Thracian mercenaries finally reached Europe. Here they discovered that the two main Thracian kingdoms were at war against each other and soon found further employment in the ongoing conflict (which ended with the expansion of one realm at the expense of the other).

Following the end of the violent civil war that shattered the Persian Empire, the Thracians of Bithynia tried to regain their independence by revolting against the Achaemenid satrap who governed their territory. By 390 BC, Bithynia was still part of the Persian Empire but had obtained a high degree of autonomy. The following decades of Thracian history can be considered a 'golden age' for the tribes settled in present-day Bulgaria, since their communities lived through a great demographical expansion and flourished from an economic point of view. Two tribes in particular assumed a prominent role during this new historical phase: the Triballi, who conquered large territories in the heart of the Balkans at the expense of the Macedonians, and the Getae. The latter were settled around the Danube delta, in north-eastern Thrace, where they lived in a constant state of war against the Scythians and became famous as horse-breeders. The cavalry of the Getae had much in common with that of the nomadic peoples settled in Scythia and was considered to be the best in Thrace. At the peak of their expansion, the Getae occupied a portion of territory located north of the Danube, which had long been held by the Scythians. Most of the Greeks did not consider the Getae to be part of the Thracian tribes, because they had been heavily influenced by the Scythians from a cultural point of view and also had a distinct religion that was quite different from that of the other Thracians. Despite this, the social structures and the main traditions of the Getae were clearly Thracian. During this golden age, the Thracian political scene continued to be dominated by the two main kingdoms that had emerged from the collapse of the Odrysian realm. One of

Thracian warrior equipped with a *labrys* axe, which was a ceremonial weapon. (*Photo and copyright by 'Ancient Thrace'*)

Panoply of a Thracian warrior. (*Photo and copyright by 'Ancient Thrace'*)

these was ruled from 383–359 BC by a capable war leader named Kotys, who was able to unify the two main Thracian states after decades of political fragmentation. Kotys had at his service the skilful Athenian general Iphicrates, who had a great knowledge of Thracian culture and warfare. Iphicrates was heavily influenced by Thracian light infantry tactics, which were the starting point for his famous reform of the traditional hoplite equipment. Iphicrates had been exiled from his city despite having obtained some brilliant victories, but soon found a new home in Thrace; he even married Kotys' daughter and was given two coastal cities by the Thracian monarch as a reward for his loyalty.

The Thracian golden age came to an end in 359 BC, when Kotys was assassinated during a conspiracy that had been organized by the Athenians. The Athenians feared (correctly) that the Thracians could attack and conquer all their allied cities located on the Thracian coastline, as demonstrated by the military events of 376 BC which saw a major Thracian offensive against the Greek colony of Abdera. After Kotys' death, the Thracian realm was divided into three parts between his three sons; in that same year, Philip II ascended to the throne of Macedonia. In 357 BC, the hostilities between the Thracians and the Athenians – which had been continuing for many years – finally came to an end and Athens concluded treaties of alliance with the three new kings. The political and military situation of the southern Balkans, however, was about to change completely due to the emergence of Macedonia as a significant regional power. When Philip II of the Argead dynasty became King of Macedonia in 359 BC, at the age of 23, his country was by no means an important actor on the Greek political stage. Macedonia was located on the northern borders of the Greek world, and thus was considered a semi-civilized kingdom by most of the Greek city-states. In effect, the Macedonian state had originated as a tribal kingdom that was not very different from the smaller ones that were located around it. Over the centuries, the Macedonians had progressively adopted Greek culture, but their tribal origins were still clearly visible in their political and social structures. One of the key features of the Macedonians was their innate propensity for war: this was the result of centuries of open conflict against the neighbouring tribes living in the central Balkans (including the Thracians). More or less every year, the Macedonian state was under attack from one of its local enemies, who were able to conduct guerrilla operations with great success and for long periods. In addition, the Kingdom of Macedonia was continuously influenced in its internal politics by interference from the most powerful Greek city-states (in particular Sparta, which was the main ally of the Macedonians for several decades before the ascendancy of Philip II).

The new Macedonian king had spent part of his youth as a royal hostage in Thebes, and thus had learned the Greek art of war. Despite being very young, he had a clear plan to transform Macedonia into a military power by reforming its armed forces. Philip II's innovations led to the birth of the famous Macedonian phalanx and the organization of a formidable heavy cavalry force that had no rivals in the Balkans. With his new army, the Macedonian king could stabilize his frontiers and submit the warlike Illyrians and Thracians living on his borders. Understanding that Philip could represent a deadly menace for their interests, the Athenians organized a strong anti-Macedonian coalition in 356 BC that comprised one of the Thracian kingdoms as well as other allies such as the Illyrians and the Paeonians. This military alliance, however, proved too weak and was only short-lived. Philip defeated it very easily and

Personal equipment of a Thracian warrior. (*Photo and copyright by 'Ancient Thrace'*)

Points of Thracian spear and javelins. (*Photo and copyright by 'Ancient Thrace'*)

Thracian knife with a curved blade and *kopis* sword. (*Photo and copyright by 'Ancient Thrace'*)

acquired control over the gold mines of Pangaion, which until that time had always been exploited by the tribes of south-western Thrace. In 347 BC, the Macedonian king launched his first Thracian campaign, but did not achieve decisive results. The Thracians, like the Illyrians, proved to be tough enemies for the Macedonians thanks to their unique combat skills and knowledge of the territory over which the campaign was fought. During the following years, Philip II conducted several wars against the Thracian tribes; by 341 BC, most of his initial objectives had been accomplished. The Thracians no longer represented a serious menace to the stability of his kingdom, while in addition, he was able to annex southern Thrace to his realm. In 339 BC, however, the Thracians took their revenge, attacking the Macedonian Army while it was returning home after conducting a campaign against the Scythians on the Danube. The Triballi attacked and defeated the Macedonian troops, and during the clash Philip was badly wounded and it was feared he may die. The Macedonian king recovered, but did not have time to launch a punitive invasion against the Triballi because his attention was drawn to the south. The following year he fought the decisive Battle of Chaeronea against the Athenian and Theban military forces in order to obtain complete political dominance over Greece.

When Philip II was assassinated in 336 BC, his young son Alexander became King of Macedon. The Thracians revolted against the new monarch as soon as they knew that their mortal enemy Philip had died. As a result, one of Alexander's first acts as king was to put down the Thracian rebellion. He rapidly invaded Thracian lands and moved north to fight against the Triballi, his main opponents in the region. The Triballi were heavily defeated by Alexander during a violent pitched battle, which saw the participation of the Macedonian phalanx and heavy cavalry. The Triballi were superior to Alexander's light troops, but the new infantry and 'Companion' cavalry of the Macedonian king proved unstoppable against the Thracians. After crushing the Triballi and forcing them to move north of the Danube, Alexander attacked the Getae elsewhere along the northern border. The Getae had moved north of the Danube with their army, in order to put a natural barrier between them and the Macedonians. Alexander, however, quickly crossed the river and organized a surprise attack against his Thracian foes. The Getae were decisively defeated and obliged to move north into the territory of Scythae. In an extremely rapid and effective campaign, Alexander had been able to secure the northern borders of his realm and had conclusively beaten the two most important Thracian tribes. When he started the invasion of the Persian Empire, which transformed him into Alexander the Great, the recently subdued Thracians made a major contribution to the formation of his expeditionary force. They provided the following contingents to the Macedonian Army: three squadrons of light cavalry with a total of 900 horsemen, 7,000 light infantrymen and 1,000 archers. Of the three cavalry squadrons one was sent by the Paeonians and two by the Odrysians. In addition, it is important to note that an entire component of the Macedonian Army was recruited from the territories of southern Thrace that were annexed to Macedonia by Philip II. This was the corps of the Prodromoi, or 'Scouts', which consisted of four light cavalry squadrons with a total of 800 horsemen. These were excellent mounted skirmishers, as were the soldiers of the other three Thracian squadrons, but were under the orders of Macedonian officers since they were not allied troops (the Prodromoi were part of the 'national' Macedonian Army).

The Thracians of Alexander's army played a crucial role in the difficult battles fought against the Persians. They were undoubtedly the best light cavalrymen and light infantrymen in the Macedonian military forces thanks to their great combat skills. The mounted troops conducted reconnaissance operations and could cover long distances in a very short time; the foot contingents, on the other hand, usually opened all Alexander's pitched battles by throwing their missile weapons and were of great use to protect the exposed flanks of the phalanx. A further 500 Thracian light cavalrymen joined Alexander's army after the Persian expedition had already started. Then in 325 BC, two years before Alexander the Great's death, another 5,000 Thracian mounted soldiers were sent to Asia.

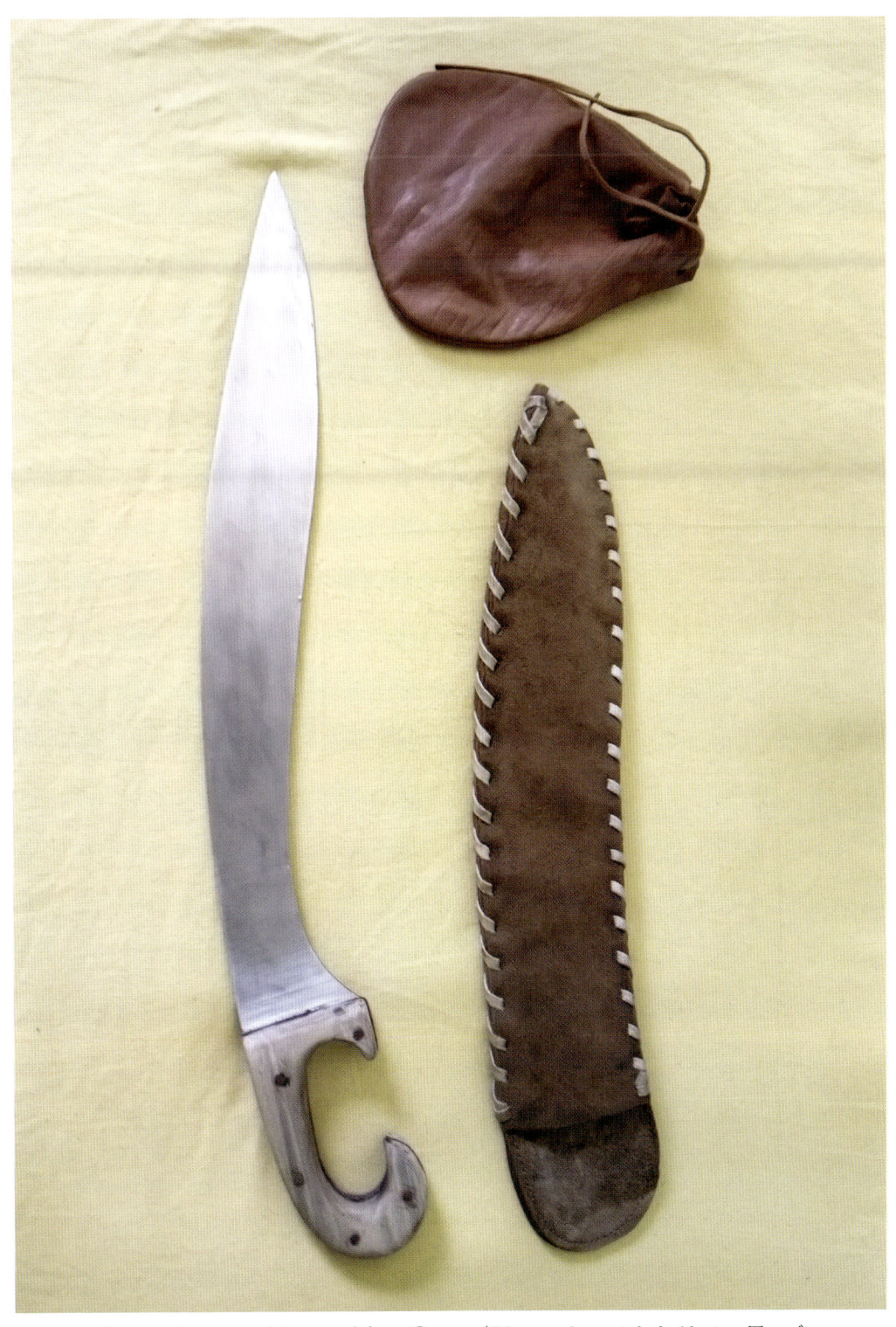

The Thracian 'golden age' and the Rise of Macedonia 47

Thracian *kopis* sword imported from Greece. (*Photo and copyright by 'Ancient Thrace'*)

Thracian *kopis* sword. (*Photo and copyright by 'Ancient Thrace'*)

Chapter 4

Hellenistic Thrace

The governor of Thrace in 323 BC was Lysimachus, a Macedonian general of Thessalian descent who had served for many years under Alexander's direct orders. By the time of Alexander the Great's death, the Macedonian situation in Thrace was a tricky one. A few years before, the previous governor of the region had launched a large military campaign against the Scythians with all the troops that were available in Thrace. This turned out to be a complete disaster, causing around 30,000 Macedonian casualties. As a result of these events, the Macedonian garrison of Thrace had been reduced to just 4,000 infantry and 2,000 cavalry, by no means sufficient to keep order among the warlike Thracian tribes, which were ready to revolt at the first opportunity. Imposing any kind of rule over Thrace would have not been easy for Lysimachus, especially as the Macedonian presence in the region was not a uniform one: southern Thrace was formally part of the Kingdom of Macedonia, but northern Thrace was made up of semi-independent tribal kingdoms that were client states of the Macedonians. Consequently, the governor of Thrace could exert direct dominance over just one portion of the country. Soon after Lysimachus' arrival, the Odrysians and several other client communities revolted against the Macedonians in the hope of regaining their former independence. This new Thracian rebellion was particularly violent and Lysimachus experienced great difficulty in crushing it. He was vastly outnumbered by the enemy and was forced to fight a large pitched battle against the Thracians. This, against all odds, ended up as a victory for the Macedonians, despite the very large losses suffered by Lysimachus' men. After these events, by 320 BC, the Macedonian general had secured control over Thrace and could rule the region as one of the several independent kingdoms that had been created after the collapse of Alexander the Great's empire.

Among the various 'diadochi' (i.e. successor kings), Lysimachus was the one who experienced most difficulties in keeping control over his own realm. He had to face several internal revolts, and at the same time was involved in many of the conflicts that shaped the political map of the Mediterranean after Alexander's death in 323 BC. From the outset, Lysimachus' main political aim was to conquer Anatolia: he had in mind to create a large kingdom that could control the Dardanelles Straits and the Bosphorus between Europe and Asia. To do this, he would have had to defeat one

Thracian *pelte* shield. (*Photo and copyright by 'Ancient Thrace'*)

Thracian *pelte* shield and *kopis* swords. (*Photo and copyright by 'Ancient Thrace'*)

of the most famous diadochi, Antigonus Monophtalmus, who ruled over a large portion of western Asia – including Anatolia – and had strong military forces at his command. In 315 BC, Lysimachus joined a military coalition that was organized to defeat Antigonus. This comprised the Kingdom of Macedonia ruled by Cassander, the Kingdom of Egypt under Ptolemy and the Seleucid Empire ruled by Seleucus. Lysimachus' contribution to this military alliance, however, was only minor because he had to face a serious revolt of the northern Thracian tribes that also involved the Schytians. In addition, he had to crush a rebellion of the Greek colonies located on the Black Sea coast of Thrace. In 309 BC, Lysimachus built a capital for his Thracian realm, which was named Lysimachia; this was located in a strategic position on the neck connecting Thracian Chersonese with the mainland. Building a capital on the Dardanelles was a clear demonstration of Lysimachus's great political ambitions. A second military coalition against Antigonus was formed in 302 BC, and once again Lysimachus joined it; on this occasion, however, his participation in the ensuing conflict was much more significant. He entered Anatolia at the head of his army and of some allied troops sent by Cassander. When Antigonus moved against him, Lysimachus opted to retreat and await the arrival of further reinforcements. After extra troops (commanded by Seleucus) reached Anatolia in 301 BC, a decisive battle between Lysimachus and Antigonus was fought at Ipsus. The clash was a triumph for the allies, with Antigonus killed in battle. After Ipsus, Lysimachus could finally obtain Anatolia as he had long planned, while the rest of Antigonus' Asian kingdom was given to the Seleucid Empire.

As a result of these events, after several centuries, the Thracians of Europe and those of Asia were finally reunited into a single state that was centred on the Dardanelles Straits. Both Phrygia and Bithynia were part of Lysimachus' new territories in Anatolia. During the following years, the Thracian ruler tried to expand his dominions north of the Danube by attacking the Getae, but this campaign proved a complete failure. Lysimachus was captured by the enemy and was released only after giving back to the Getae all the lands that he had temporarily conquered north of the Danube. Meanwhile, the political situation in Macedonia had changed: the kingdom was no longer ruled by Cassander, but was now under the control of Demetrius, son of Antigonus Monophtalmus. The new Macedonian monarch was obviously hostile to Lysimachus, attacking his realm while he was fighting in the north against the Getae. In 287 BC, after forming an alliance with Pyrrhus of Epirus, Lysimachus invaded Macedonia and expelled Demetrius from the country. Soon after, however, the two allies who had defeated Antigonus' son started to quarrel between themselves for possession of Macedonia. In 285 BC, Lysimachus was able to defeat Pyrrhus of Epirus and obtained complete control over the Kingdom of Macedonia. Although he had reached the peak of his personal power, serious problems soon started to appear on the horizon. Lysimachus was by now quite old, and thus inside his court an unofficial war of succession began. Among the internecine participants was a foreign pretender, Ptolemy Keraunos, who was the son of Ptolemy I, King of Egypt. Hoping to use the internal fragmentation of Lysimachus' court to his advantage, Seleucus took the opportunity to invade Lysimachus' territories in Anatolia to complete his conquest of Hellenistic Asia. The decisive battle between Lysimachus and Seleucus was fought at Corupedium in 281 BC, the last great clash of the Diadochi Wars that had begun four decades earlier. The battle was particularly violent and ended with victory for Seleucus, Lysimachus being killed in combat.

After Corupedium, Seleucus rapidly annexed Anatolia to his Seleucid Empire and then crossed the sea to also conquer Thrace and Macedonia. He dreamed of reuniting all the European and Asian territories that had formerly been part of Alexander the Great's empire. Ptolemy Keraunos had joined Seleucus at the beginning of the war that ended with the Battle of Corupedium, but when his new protector crossed the Hellespont he assassinated the Seleucid ruler in order to claim Thrace and Macedonia for himself. Ptolemy Keraunos rapidly moved to Lysimachia, where he was acclaimed king by the Seleucid troops that had now joined his cause. As a result of these events, Macedonia and Thrace continued to be ruled by the same monarch. Ptolemy Keraunos did his best to secure his new royal title, forming a strong military alliance with Pyrrhus of Epirus (he even provided Pyrrhus with numerous troops and war elephants for his famous invasion of Italy). In 279 BC, however, matters took a completely unexpected turn: a large number of Celts, coming from Central Europe, invaded the Balkans in search of new lands to raid and conquer. The arrival of these strangers was taken as an opportunity by the Thracian tribes, who had resented Ptolemy Keraunos' rule from the beginning and considered the new king a usurper. Consequently, instead of fighting to defend their lands, the Thracians allied themselves with the invading Celts. Ptolemy Keraunos tried to stop the Celts in Macedonia, but was defeated and killed by the northern barbarians. After his death, the Thracian tribes regained their independence and any form of Hellenistic state ceased to exist in Thrace. Macedonia remained in a state of complete political chaos for two years before a new dynasty could assume control. Meanwhile, the march of the Celts continued south, towards Greece. During 279 and 278 BC they raided much of the Greek countryside, before being halted at the Thermopylae Pass by the forces of Antigonus Gonatas, the future King of Macedon. The Celts, however, were able to turn the strategic pass without fighting the superior forces opposing them, and continued their advance towards southern Greece. Even Delphi and its famous sanctuary were raided by the invaders, who seemed impossible to defeat. Eventually,

Thracian sling. (Photo and copyright by 'Ancient Thrace')

after having plundered much of the region, the Celts left Greece, but some of them settled in the heart of Anatolia.

After the death of Alexander the Great, the Thracians of Asia endured varying destinies. Phrygia remained part of the Seleucid Empire until most of its territory was occupied by the Celts who arrived in Anatolia after pillaging Greece. The Phrygians were obliged to become subjects of the newcomers, who destroyed the ancient city of Gordium and created their new Kingdom of Galatia. Bithynia, meanwhile, regained its independence even before 323 BC and remained an autonomous kingdom during most of the Hellenistic period. None of the diadochi realms were able to occupy it permanently. Both Lysimachus and Antigonus tried to conquer Bithynia, but they were never able to overcome the resistance of the region's warriors, who were masters of fighting in the difficult terrain upon which they lived. In 297 BC, the ruler of independent Bithynia assumed the title of 'basileus' (i.e. king), and his realm was officially recognized as a fully autonomous state. Following Lysimachus' death, Anatolia became fragmented into a series of small independent kingdoms, among which Bithynia was one of the most stable. The local royal family founded a new capital at Nicomedia, which soon became a prosperous city and one of Asia Minor's most important commercial centres. Nicomedes I, ascending to the Bithynian throne

Thracian *alopekis*, commonly known as the 'Phrygian cap'. (*Photo and copyright by 'Ancient Thrace'*)

in 280 BC, was the first monarch to launch a significant process of 'hellenization' inside his realm from a military point of view: until then, the Bithynians had continued to fight as light infantrymen, like the Thracians of Europe. Under Nicomedes I, the Bithynian warriors started to be re-equipped as Hellenistic-style *thureophoroi* (light infantrymen with oval shields) and progressively abandoned their Thracian military traditions. During larger military campaigns, these were usually supplemented by contingents of mercenaries contracted in Thrace or Galatia. Apparently, some of the later Bithynian kings had a personal bodyguard formed by 500 Thracian mercenaries from Europe. Bithynian mounted troops included both light horsemen (a sort of mounted *thureophoroi*) and heavy cavalry (the nobility of the country). In 74 BC, the last monarch of Bithynia, having no direct heirs, bequeathed his kingdom to the Roman Republic.

In addition to Bithynia, there were another three minor independent states in Anatolia during the second phase of the Hellenistic period: the kingdoms of Pergamon, Cappadocia and Galatia. Pergamon originated from Lysimachus' possessions in Anatolia, which initially became part of the Seleucid Empire but were later organized as an autonomous kingdom by one of Lysimachus' officers, Philetaerus. The latter chose as his capital the city of Pergamon but never claimed formal independence for his new realm; officially, he remained a vassal of the Seleucids. Over time, however, it became clear that the Kingdom of Pergamon was a fully autonomous state. Eumenes I, the successor of Philetaerus, was the first monarch of Pergamon to proclaim the independence of his kingdom. In the following decades, the Attalids (the dynasty ruling over Pergamon) fought several wars against the Seleucids, particularly for possession of southern Anatolia, and despite being much smaller than their enemies, they were successful on several occasions. Once Rome became involved in the politics of the Hellenistic world, the Kingdom of Pergamon became the most loyal and important ally of the Republic. The last Attalid king, Attalus III, died without an heir in 133 BC: in order to prevent the outbreak of a civil war that would have destroyed his realm, he bequeathed the whole of Pergamon to the Roman Republic. As a result, Rome obtained most of Anatolia without a fight and could form its new province of Asia. The southern portion of Phrygia that was never occupied by the Celts of Galatia remained part of Pergamon during the whole period taken into account. The independent Kingdom of Cappadocia was founded in 331 BC by Ariarathes, the last Persian governor of the Cappadocian Satrapy. Since the Macedonians continued their advance towards the heart of the Persian Empire without attacking Cappadocia, Ariarathes was able to retain power in his own province and avoided a direct confrontation with the army of Alexander the Great. Ariarathes was eventually defeated and killed by Perdiccas in 322 BC, but after

Thracian *zeira* cloak. (*Photo and copyright by 'Ancient Thrace'*)

Thracian *embades* boots. (*Photo and copyright by 'Ancient Thrace'*)

a brief period of Macedonian occupation, Cappadocia became independent again in 301 BC under Ariarathes' son. The new monarch initiated a new dynasty that was to last until 96 BC, when Mithridates VI of Pontus invaded Cappadocia and briefly annexed it to his possessions. After defeating Pontus, the Romans decided to install a new dynasty in Cappadocia and transformed the minor realm into one of their client kingdoms. In 36 BC, the last monarch of Cappadocia died without heirs and thus the Romans gave Cappadocia to a local noble named Archelaus, who was a personal friend of the triumvir Marcus Antonius. When Archelaus died in AD 17, Cappadocia was absorbed into the Roman Empire.

The Celts settling in Anatolia belonged to three different tribes: the Tectosages, the Trocmi and the Tolistobogii. These, as mentioned above, established themselves on the plateau of Phrygia after defeating the local inhabitants of Thracian descent. During the early phase of their settlement, the Celts of Asia mostly supported themselves by plundering bordering countries or by serving as mercenaries in the various Hellenistic armies of the time. In 232 BC, the Attalids of Pergamon defeated the Galatians in battle, which led to the creation of a more permanent Galatian state in central Anatolia that became a vassal of Pergamon. In 189 BC, the Romans launched a major expedition against the Celts of Asia that became known as the Galatian War. After being defeated, the Galatians lost much of their military power and were later invaded by Mithridates VI of Pontus. Thanks to the decisive help of the Romans, however, the Celts of Anatolia were later able to regain their independence after the end of the Mithridatic Wars (88–63 BC) that were fought between Pontus and the Roman Republic. Galatia formally became a client state of Rome in 62 BC, and in 25 BC it was finally annexed by the Romans.

In Thrace, following Ptolemy Keraunos' death, the local tribes regained their independence and remained at the margins of the Hellenistic world for most of the following decades. During this period, the tribes of central Thrace had to fight against a Celtic community that had remained in their territory after the great Celtic invasion. Some warriors from Central Europe had settled in Thrace, where they built a small independent kingdom around Tylis. The Thracians fought with all their resources against the newcomers, and by 212 BC the Celtic community living in central Thrace had been destroyed. During the years 278–200 BC, the Thracians experienced a new age of prosperity and remained free from the political influence of the various states located around them, despite being under the formal 'political protection' of Macedonia. This situation came to an end when the interests of Macedonia collided with the expansionist ambitions of the Roman Republic.

Warrior of the Scordisci armed with spear and shield. (*Photo and copyright by 'Ancient Thrace'*)

Warrior of the Scordisci equipped with spear and shield. (*Photo and copyright by 'Ancient Thrace'*)

Chapter 5

The Roman Conquest of Thrace

The first conflict between the Roman Republic and the Kingdom of Macedonia started in 217 BC, while the Romans were already fighting against Hannibal and the Carthaginians during the Second Punic War. The second conflict with Carthage was particularly dramatic for Rome, involving Hannibal's invasion of Italy and several heavy defeats for the legions. Trying to take advantage of the ongoing military difficulties of Rome, the Macedonians decided to attack the Republic while most of its legions were facing Hannibal. Philip V, King of Macedon, opened hostilities with Rome after the legions were utterly defeated at the Battle of the Lake Trasimene in June 217 BC. With the Carthaginian army seemingly running amok across Italy, the Macedonian monarch was sure that the Romans would be too busy to oppose his plans to conquer continental Greece and the Illyrian territories of the northern Balkans. During the preceding decades, the Roman Republic had already fought two victorious conflicts against the Illyrians and thus had reached the borders of Macedonia; in addition, the Romans had gradually obtained naval dominance over the Adriatic Sea. These expansionist moves were clearly unacceptable for the Macedonians, who considered the whole Balkans as part of their sphere of influence. The First Macedonian War started with a Macedonian invasion of the Illyrian territories on the Adriatic coast. For the first time in their history, the Macedonians built a large fleet, consisting of more than 100 warships, and disembarked their forces in Illyria. The ensuing land campaign, however, was a complete failure for Philip V, who achieved very little. In the summer of 215 BC, after the Romans had been crushed by the Carthaginians at the momentous Battle of Cannae, the Macedonians sent ambassadors to southern Italy in order to negotiate a military alliance with Hannibal. On their way back to Macedonia, the emissaries of Philip were captured by the Romans, who thereby learned of the new alliance between Carthage and Macedonia from the official documents that they were transporting. In 214 BC, a Macedonian army tried again to invade Illyria, but this time the Romans were able to disembark troops on the Balkan coast to oppose Philip's offensive. Despite facing greater numbers, the Roman legions were able to defeat the Macedonians and restore Rome's influence over Illyria. Philip V was obliged to abandon his expansionist plans, returning to Macedonia with his forces. During the

Warrior of the Scordisci wearing a torc neck ring. (*Photo and copyright by 'Ancient Thrace'*)

following years, the Macedonians tried to penetrate Illyria from the south, while the Romans secured the area by concluding a military alliance with the Aetolian League. This was a confederation of Greek communities located on the southern borders of Macedonia, which had until recently been at war with Philip V. In 211 BC, the Aetolians allied themselves with Rome in order to fight more effectively against their common enemy, Macedonia. During the following year, the Kingdom of Pergamon also joined this anti-Macedonian alliance and sent its fleet to the Adriatic in order to support the Romans. The Macedonians had destroyed their own fleet after their first failed invasion of Illyria, having had no further use for it, so the allies controlled the Adriatic Sea without hindrance. The Macedonians fought in mainland Greece against the Aetolians for several years, obtaining the support of the Achaean League (another confederation of Greek communities and the mortal enemy of the Aetolian League). In 206 BC, after having suffered several heavy defeats, the Aetolians decided to make peace with Philip V: their Roman allies were heavily involved in campaigns against the Carthaginians and thus could not provide effective military support. The fleet of Pergamon had also returned to Anatolia, so the Aetolians were left to fight alone without allies. The First Macedonian War officially came to an end in 205 BC with the Treaty of Phoenice, according to which Philip V renounced his alliance with Carthage but could still exert direct influence over certain areas of Illyria. In practice, very little changed from the situation of 217 BC; it was by now clear, however, that Rome and Macedonia would fight a new war for dominance over the Balkans as soon as Hannibal could be defeated, which happened in 202 BC with the decisive Roman victory at the Battle of Zama in North Africa.

Sure enough, the Second Macedonian War broke out in 200 BC after Philip V invaded Attica and menaced the city of Athens. Advancing from their bases in Illyria, the Romans invaded Macedonia from the west but were not able to obtain a clear-cut victory over the Macedonians. In this conflict, the Roman Republic was again supported by the Kingdom of Pergamon and the Aetolian League: Pergamon sent its fleet and the Aetolians attacked Macedonia from the south. In 198 BC, after several months of inconclusive operations, the Romans landed in the Balkans with a substantial army. The Roman expeditionary force was able to achieve an initial victory in Epirus, at the Battle of the Aous, but the clash did not prove decisive. Meanwhile, at sea, the allied fleet of Rome and Pergamon reinforced Athens, which convinced the Achaean League to join the anti-Macedonian alliance. During the winter of 198–197 BC, the opposing sides tried to find a compromise in order to bring the hostilities to an end, but the peace negotiations came to nothing. The decisive clash of the Second Macedonian War was fought at Cynoscephalae in 197 BC. Here, for the first time on Greek soil, the famed Macedonian phalanx faced the Roman legions, with 26,000 Romans defeating 25,000 Macedonians. The battle took place on hilly terrain, where Philip V's heavy infantry did not have enough space to manoeuvre effectively: this greatly advantaged the flexible Roman legions, which resisted the enemy charge and used their missile weapons (javelins) in devastating fashion. After this defeat, having also suffered significant losses on other secondary fronts, the Macedonian king decided he had no option but to make peace with Rome. Under the terms of the subsequent agreement, the Macedonians were forced to remove all their garrisons that were scattered across Greece and – for the first time since the age of Philip II – were obliged to acknowledge the political freedom of the Greek cities. Philip V also had to pay a large war indemnity and was made to surrender all his naval forces. The Macedonian Army, meanwhile, was reduced to just 5,000 soldiers and was officially forbidden from having war elephants. Thanks to their victory in the Second Macedonian War, the Romans could present themselves as the saviours of Greek freedom, yet all they had done was simply replace Macedonian predominance over Greece with their own.

Philip V died in 179 BC and his ambitious son, Perseus, became King of Macedon. Perseus had great plans for the expansion of his realm, his main objective being to restore Macedonia's ancient glory. To achieve this goal, he spent most of his early reign trying to form a large anti-Roman alliance that comprised the Seleucid Empire as well as Greek cities, the latter having soon turned against the Romans after the Republic assumed indirect control over their territories. The Third Macedonian War duly broke out in 171 BC, the Romans once more being supported by their historical allies the Aetolian League and Pontus. While a Roman army disembarked in Greece, Macedonian forces invaded Thessaly from the north. Thessaly had been part of Macedonia's territory since it was conquered by Philip II, and Perseus could not accept that it was now free from his political influence. It was in Thessaly that the first significant clash of the Third Macedonian War was fought, at Callinicus. The battle was a significant victory for Perseus, who defeated the Romans thanks to the superiority of his cavalry and light infantry. The war, however, was not yet over. In 169 BC, the Macedonians invaded Illyria, being by now sure that their home territories could no longer be attacked from Thessaly. The Macedonian invasion of Illyria was a success: Perseus' troops conquered many enemy strongholds and captured more than 1,500 soldiers from the local Roman garrisons. During the winter of the same year, the Macedonians also invaded Aetolia, but this operation ended without achieving significant results. In the following spring, the Romans landed an army in Epirus and marched on Macedonia, but faced strong resistance during their advance across the mountains. Perseus' light infantry fought with great distinction during these operations, greatly slowing down the movement of the Roman legions, to such an extent that the Romans were not able to invade Macedonia as they had planned.

Warrior of the Scordisci armed with spear and shield. (*Photo and copyright by 'Ancient Thrace'*)

66 Armies of the Thracians and Dacians, 500 BC to AD 150

Warrior of the Scordisci equipped with slashing sword and shield. (*Photo and copyright by 'Ancient Thrace'*)

The decisive year of the Third Macedonian War was 168 BC, during which a major pitched battle was fought north of Thessaly at Pydna. The Battle of Pydna is widely recognized as one of the most important military clashes of Antiquity, which can be clearly understood by analysing the numbers of troops involved on either side. Perseus deployed his whole military potential, with 39,000 infantry and 4,000 cavalry, while the Romans confronted him with 36,000 foot troops and 2,600 mounted men. When the battle was over, Perseus had lost most of his forces, with 11,000 troops captured by the Romans. From a practical point of view, the Macedonian military potential had been broken decisively. After the defeat, Perseus retreated north to his capital of Pella with what remained of his cavalry; despite having suffered such severe losses, he was determined to continue resisting. However, the young Macedonian monarch was soon surrounded by Roman forces and had no choice but to surrender. Once captured, he was sent in chains to Rome, where he spent most of the rest of his life as a captive.

With the Third Macedonian War now over, the Romans were determined to avoid any future military resurgence by Macedonia. To that end, the Senate decided to break up the Kingdom of Macedonia into four cantons, which would be Roman protectorates. Rome now exerted control over all the natural resources of the country, in particular over its gold and silver mines. In addition, Macedonian territory was garrisoned by significant numbers of Roman troops. The peace conditions imposed by the Roman Republic were felt to be too harsh by the Macedonians, who were forced to become vassals of a foreign power after having been the dominant state of the Greek world for two centuries. Consequently, in 150 BC, a man named Andriscus, pretending to be a son of the former Macedonian king Perseus, guided a popular uprising in the four regions of Macedonia. His rebellion soon developed into a widespread conflict, which became known as the Fourth Macedonian War. Despite having only a handful of soldiers under his command, Andriscus was able to obtain several minor victories, and thus his uprising continued until 148 BC. In that year, the Romans were finally able to restore order in Macedonia by using very harsh repressive methods. Two years later, in a last desperate attempt to preserve their independence, the Greek cities of the Achaean League attacked the Romans, but were easily defeated by the legions. Roman troops besieged and destroyed Corinth in 146 BC, thus bringing to an end Greek freedom. In that same year, Macedonia was transformed into a Roman province and the Third Punic War was fought, which ended with the destruction of Carthage and the disappearance of the Carthaginians from the political scene of the Mediterranean. The fall of Corinth and the destruction of Carthage were two events that had a great symbolic impact at the time, with 146 BC marking the ascendancy of the Roman Republic as the leading power of Antiquity.

Light infantryman of the Scordisci carrying a javelin and oval shield. (*Photo and copyright by 'Ancient Thrace'*)

Warriors of the Bastarnae (left) and the Scordisci (right). (*Photo and copyright by 'Ancient Thrace'*)

The Macedonian Wars had a deep impact on the destiny of the Thracians, whose participation in the four conflicts had been significant. During the Second Macedonian War, for example, some 2,000 Thracian warriors were part of the Macedonian Army during the Battle of Cynocephalae (197 BC). With the end of hostilities in 196 BC, the

Thracians were freed from any form of Macedonian indirect rule. The various tribes, however, started to be increasingly worried about the expanding Roman military presence in the Balkans. With the defeat of Macedonia, a significant power vacuum had been created in Greece: the Romans wanted to fill this with their own legions, but the Seleucid Empire was also looking to conquer the southern portion of the Balkans. As a result, in 192 BC, hostilities broke out between the Roman Republic and the Seleucid Empire. Two years into the war, the Romans obtained a decisive victory over the Seleucids at the Battle of Magnesia in Anatolia. While returning to Greece, however, the victorious Roman legions were attacked by the Thracians, who had assembled an army of 10,000 warriors and waited for the Romans at a narrow forested pass in south-eastern Thrace. The tribal fighters attacked the Roman rearguard, which comprised a baggage full of riches that had been taken from the defeated Seleucids. The Roman rearguard was taken by surprise and routed; all its wagons were looted before the Thracians returned to their forest fastnesses prior to the arrival of Roman reinforcements. This little-known ambush was seen as a disaster by the Romans, and was something that they would never forget. While it had been a success for the Thracians, it was obviously not a decisive one for the destiny of their country.

At the outbreak of the Third Macedonian War, Perseus' forces comprised around 3,000 Thracians, who were later supplemented by another 2,000 fighters provided by the Odrysians (who were allies of Macedonia). At the Battle of Callinicus (171 BC), the Thracians in the Macedonian army secured a clear victory over the Romans: according to ancient sources, they returned from the battlefield singing, with hundreds of severed Roman heads. This was the second time that the Thracians had humiliated the Romans, but once again this Thracian success could not halt the expansionist policy of the Roman Republic. In 168 BC, a Macedonian army was soundly defeated by Rome at the Battle of Pydna, practically ending the Third Macedonian War and transforming the Macedonians into Roman vassals. At this point, with Macedonia having been conquered, the Thracians found the Roman legions at their frontier and thus feared being next in line for Rome's expansionist moves. In 150 BC, an attempt to re-establish an independent Kingdom of Macedonia having provoked the outbreak of the Fourth Macedonian War, which lasted until 148 BC, the Thracians were again part of the anti-Roman front. As we have seen, the pretender to the Macedonian throne was defeated by the Republic and Macedonia was officially transformed into a Roman province in 146 BC. From that time onward, a state of constant war existed on the border between Roman Macedonia and independent Thrace. The Romans wanted to transform the various Thracian tribes into client communities, since they considered themselves the heirs of Macedonia's political influence over Thrace. The

Duel between warriors of the Scordisci (left) and the Bastarnae (right). (*Photo and copyright by 'Ancient Thrace'*)

Thracians, of course, had no intention of accepting the Romans as their overlords, and consequently soon started to launch aggressive raids against the province of Macedonia.

During the many 'little wars' fought against the Thracians, Roman armies were defeated on several occasions and even had one of their proconsuls killed. The Thracian warriors, with their elusive skirmishing tactics and great mobility, proved very difficult opponents for the Romans, who struggled in Balkan territory which was unknown to them. From 146 BC, the Roman Republic tried to recreate some sort of unified Thracian state, in order to transform Thrace into one of its vassal kingdoms. It would have been much easier for the Romans to control a single 'puppet' kingdom instead of keeping order among many warlike tribes. Around 100 BC, a new Odrysian Kingdom was created, but this did not last for long due to the internal divisions of the Thracians (most of whom were strongly against Rome's indirect rule of their homeland). Around 30 BC, some form of Thracian Kingdom had been restored by the Romans; by this time, the Thracian tribes that were still autonomous had all accepted some form of Roman suzerainty. In 15 BC, the population of the Thracian Kingdom rose in revolt against the Romans and killed the puppet monarch who had been installed by Rome, but the rebellion was quickly crushed by the legions. Further

Celtic sword and knife. (*Photo and copyright by 'Ancient Thrace'*)

Thracian uprisings took place during the following decades as the Roman presence in present-day Bulgaria became increasingly stable. In AD 12, Rome divided the territories of Thrace into two puppet kingdoms, but even this measure did not change the situation. The two Thracian realms soon started to fight against each other, and anti-Roman uprisings continued to occur with great frequency. In AD 45, a major new rebellion erupted in Thrace, which caused the death of one of the puppet kings chosen by the Romans. To stop the endemic guerrilla warfare that was ravaging the region, Emperor Claudius decided to transform Thrace into a Roman province in AD 46. Thracian uprisings and revolts continued for several years, but without achieving significant results. Like many other peoples living around them, the Thracians had lost forever their independence and were already slowly disappearing from history. During the following centuries, they were a fundamental component of the Roman Empire's population.

Chapter 6

The Early History of the Dacians and the Rise of Burebista

Around 700 BC, some three centuries after the Dacians had become a distinct people from the Thracians, the territory of present-day Romania was invaded by the Scythians. The invaders came from the steppes of Central Asia and had already occupied vast territories in modern southern Russia and Ukraine. Differently from the Dacians, they were a nomadic population and spent most of their life moving on horseback. From a military point of view, the Scythians deployed two different types of mounted warriors: lightly armed horse archers and fully armoured heavy cavalrymen. These two components of the Scythian military forces were used on the battlefield with a high degree of effectivity, thanks to an intelligent tactical combination: the horse archers were employed to attack the enemy on the flanks by delivering thousands of arrows with their deadly composite bows, and when the opponents were all grouped in the centre, the heavy cavalry launched a mass charge. The Dacians did not know how to counter these military tactics of the Scythians, initially having no cavalry to speak of. As a result, the Scythian conquest of Dacia was quite rapid and ended with the temporary transformation of the Dacians into subjects of the steppe warriors. Around 320 BC, however, Scythian power in Dacia started to decline due to the arrival of new invaders who conquered a large part of the region: the Celts.

During the fourth century BC, while the Celts from Gaul were expanding towards Britain and Spain, those from Austria and western Hungary started to move across Eastern Europe. The main driving force of Celtic expansionism in that part of the continent was represented, at least initially, by the two large groups of the Boii and Volcae. These were not simply tribes, but confederations made up of several smaller tribal communities. Moving from Austria, the Celts completed their conquest of Hungary and advanced along the Danube in order to occupy large territories in the Carpathian region. By the end of the fourth century BC, there was a stable Celtic presence in present-day Czech Republic, Slovakia, Hungary and south-western Poland. At this point the Celts decided to move further south and east, following two different routes. The first one crossed the territories of modern Slovenia and Croatia, in the northern part of the western Balkans, where the Celtic tribes faced the Illyrians, who tried to resist with all their energies despite being outnumbered

Celtic shield of the Scordisci. (*Photo and copyright by 'Ancient Thrace'*)

by the northern invaders. The second route followed the Danube and was directed to the Black Sea, running across Transylvania (the western part of modern Romania) and reaching the western part of present-day Ukraine. The Celtic presence in Dacia soon became quite significant, but the newcomers always had to co-exist with the local population, as the Scythians had done before them. This situation continued until 150 BC, when the Dacians started to fight against the Celtic communities in their territories in an attempt to expel them from Transylvania. This was not a simple process, because the Celts had firmly established themselves in Dacia; the Dacians, however, were supported in their long struggle by the powerful Thracian tribe of the Getae (who controlled a portion of territory north of the Danube). The violent conflict between the Dacians and Celts came to a critical point around 60 BC, when a great war leader emerged from the tribes of Dacia: Burebista. He guided the Dacians in the decisive moment of the conflict against the Celts and expelled them from the middle Danube region. Soon after achieving his objectives, Burebista was crowned as overlord of the Dacians and started to unify all the tribes of his people into some sort of centralized state. This move developed quite rapidly, thanks to the great personal capabilities of Burebista, who ordered the construction of a system of hill forts across Dacia in order to control the territories of the various communities and gradually absorbed the powerful Getae inside his political sphere of influence. Until 40 BC, he continued to fight on the borders of his new state against the Boii, who still represented a potential menace for Dacia and launched raids against Burebista's lands. During this period, however, the Dacians were also at war with another two peoples: the Bastarnae and the Scordisci.

The Bastarnae were a large tribe of mixed Celtic-Germanic descent, which originally settled in present-day Moldova before moving south towards the heart of the Balkans around 200 BC. The Bastarnae crossed the Danube in great numbers in 179 BC, having been invited to do so by Philip V of Macedon. Philip had recently been defeated by the Romans during the Second Macedonian War and had been obliged by the victors to significantly reduce the size of his armed forces. This caused serious problems to Macedonia, the new army being too small to effectively defend the eastern borders of the realm from the regular attacks by the Illyrian and Thracian tribes. To resolve this issue, Philip V intended to settle the Bastarnae on his eastern frontier as military colonists, providing defence for the area from enemy raids and being loyal subjects of the Macedonians. In addition, in case of a new war against Rome (which was very probable), they could be employed as a significant part of the Macedonian Army. The Bastarnae accepted Philip's offer and started to migrate south, but while on the march they learned that the Macedonian king had died and that they were no longer expected in their new homeland. At this point they decided to raid and pillage

Celtic shield of the Scordisci. (*Photo and copyright by 'Ancient Thrace'*)

The Early History of the Dacians and the Rise of Burebista 77

Warrior of the Bastarnae armed with spear and hexagonal shield. (*Photo and copyright by 'Ancient Thrace'*)

Thrace, the region in which they had stopped. The hostilities between the Bastarnae and the Thracians were particularly violent: the newcomers besieged various Thracian strongholds, but without success, and were later ambushed on several occasions by the Thracians. At this point, half of the Bastarnae decided to return north to their homeland, while the remainder – some 30,000 strong – remained on the eastern frontier of Macedonia. Philip V's successor, Perseus, allowed the Bastarnae to settle on the territory of the Illyrian/Thracian tribes that attacked Macedonia's eastern frontier. These tribes assaulted the winter camp that had been built by the Bastarnae, but were repulsed with heavy losses. The conflict continued with an offensive by the Bastarnae, but this ended in failure when the Celtic-Germanic warriors were massacred in an ambush. The Bastarnae had little knowledge of their new homeland, and thus were greatly exposed to ambushes when moving in large numbers; but during pitched battles, they were a match for any possible enemy. Having lost their entire baggage and supplies during the ambush, they had no choice but to return to their homelands in Moldova. Many of them died while crossing the frozen Danube on foot and others were killed by the local tribes who attacked them. Some decades after these events, the Bastarnae were gradually able to recover from the losses suffered during their failed migration. They soon found themselves at war with the expanding Dacian Kingdom of Burebista, who wanted to unify all the peoples living along the eastern part of the Danube under his personal rule and had in mind to attack the Romans in Macedonia in order to expel them from the region. To do this, he wanted to obtain the decisive military support of the Bastarnae, whom most contemporary observers considered to be the best warriors in the Balkans. Hostilities between the Dacians and the Bastarnae did not last for long, ending in victory for Burebista: the Celtic-Germanic warriors then became allies of the Dacians and contributed to the further enlargement of Burebista's army.

The Scordisci, meanwhile, were a Celtic tribe originally settled in modern Hungary, which had participated to the great Celtic invasion of the Balkans that included the sacking of much of Greece. During their march home after the expedition, the Scordisci decided to stop in the mouth of the River Sava and to build some new settlements there. Philip V of Macedon developed a very good relationship with them, since he intended to use these Celts as allies against the Illyrian/Thracian tribes and Rome (exactly like the Bastarnae). The Scordisci soon became a significant regional power in the central Balkans: they built two fortresses to protect their new territory and submitted several of the local tribes, including the Paeonians. After the transformation of Macedonia into a Roman province in 146 BC, the Scordisci were constantly at war against the Romans and launched frequent incursions into enemy territory. In 135 BC, the Romans secured their first victory over the Scordisci,

The Early History of the Dacians and the Rise of Burebista   79

Warrior of the Bastarnae equipped with spear and hexagonal shield. (*Photo and copyright by 'Ancient Thrace'*)

80 Armies of the Thracians and Dacians, 500 BC to AD 150

Warrior of the Bastarnae carrying a javelin and small shield. (*Photo and copyright by 'Ancient Thrace'*)

but in 114 BC an entire Roman expeditionary force (commanded by Gaius Porcius Cato) was destroyed by them. Another two campaigns followed in 112 and 107 BC, but the Romans were unable to expel the Celts from the mountains of present-day western Serbia. In 88 BC, the Roman Republic organized a large military expedition against the Scordisci, who had even pillaged Delphi in Greece during recent years. This time the Romans obtained a clear victory and the power of the Scordisci in the central Balkans was definitively crushed. They had no choice but to move north of the Danube in search of new lands to settle. From 55–50 BC, they found themselves at war with the Dacian Kingdom of Burebista, who wanted to transform them into his subjects or allies. The Dacians eventually emerged victorious from this conflict, and the Scordisci, like the Getae and Bastarnae, also came under the political influence of Burebista. After having secured control over most of the eastern Balkans, Burebista developed an aggressive attitude towards Roman Macedonia and launched several raids against the Illyrian/Thracian tribes living on his southern borders. The Dacians also started to attack the Greek colonies that were located on their Black Sea coastline from about 55 BC. These were conquered one by one, something that the Thracians had never been able to achieve in the south. The Romans did very little to oppose Dacian expansionism during this phase, being heavily involved on other fronts. Julius Caesar was completing the conquest of Gaul, and there was the strong possibility of a civil war between him and Pompey. Civil war duly erupted in 49 BC and affected the whole Mediterranean, since each state bordering the Roman Republic was forced to take a position in favour of Caesar or Pompey. Burebista decided to support Pompey, but the great Roman general was defeated and killed before he could send any military contingent into Roman Macedonia. Caesar was well aware of the Dacians' military potential and considered Burebista as a dangerous enemy. After becoming the sole ruler of Rome, he started planning a major punitive expedition against Dacia but was assassinated in 44 BC before the proposed campaign could be launched. Some months after Julius Caesar's death, Burebista was also killed during a plot organized by the Dacian aristocracy, which resented the new centralized form of government introduced by Burebista and feared the possibility of an armed conflict with Rome. Soon after these events, the Dacian Kingdom collapsed and was broken up into several smaller realms that soon started to quarrel among themselves. All the great political achievements of Burebista were lost and a new phase in the history of the Dacians began.

Warrior of the Bastarnae armed with spear and hexagonal shield. (*Photo and copyright by 'Ancient Thrace'*)

Chapter 7

The First War with Rome and the Rise of Decebalus

Following Burebista's death, the Dacians no longer represented a menace for the Romans. Their large kingdom was now fragmented into several parts and the great multi-national army created by Burebista, numbering around 100,000 warriors, no longer existed. The Roman Republic abandoned Caesar's plans for an invasion of Dacia and limited itself to keeping order on the Balkan frontier. This situation started to change only in AD 69 with the emergence of a new Dacian leader named Duras. Until the end of Augustus' reign in AD 14, Dacia continued to be divided into five smaller kingdoms that could all be easily controlled by the Romans. In the following decades, however, a new sense of national identity started to emerge among the Dacian communities. Rome was increasingly perceived as a deadly menace, and thus all Dacians felt the need for a joint action against them. Duras became king in AD 69, after his father Scorilo was probably killed during a Dacian raid launched against the Roman province of Moesia. The province had been created by the Romans during Augustus' reign as a buffer zone between Macedonia and Dacia. Moesia was located to the north of Macedonia and south-west of Dacia. Before the Romans' arrival, the region was inhabited by the Moesi (a tribe of Dacian stock), the Triballi (a Thracian tribe) and a portion of the Bastarnae. The Romans considered Moesia a key region and decided to conquer it in order to protect Macedonia from the incursions of the 'barbarians' living north of the Danube. The northern border of the new province was in fact marked by the course of the great river. The *casus belli* for the invasion of Moesia was provided to the Romans by the Bastarnae, who attacked one of their allied Thracian tribes. During the ensuing conflict, thousands of Bastarnae were killed by the Romans and the Moesi were also forced to submit. Before more reinforcements sent by the northern Bastarnae could move south of the Danube, the Romans had already completed the conquest of Moesia, that was transformed into one of their provinces in AD 6. The Dacians never accepted Rome's conquest of Moesia and soon started to attack the region with rapid incursions. That organized by Scorilo in AD 69 was the first major raid, but ended in failure.

After Scorilo's death, Duras became king and continued the policy of his predecessor. He started to rebuild the military power of the Dacians and strove to reunify the various tribes of his people. Duras assembled a large army in AD 85

84   Armies of the Thracians and Dacians, 500 BC to AD 150

Warrior of the Bastarnae equipped with spear and hexagonal shield. (*Photo and copyright by 'Ancient Thrace'*)

The First War with Rome and the Rise of Decebalus

and invaded the Roman province of Moesia from the north. The attack enjoyed great initial success, with the Romans unable to stop the Dacians. An entire legion was annihilated by the invaders and the governor of Moesia, Oppius Sabinus, was beheaded during the critical battle of this campaign. At this point it became clear in Rome that something had changed in Dacia: there was now a strong enemy leader in that sector of the frontier, who had the necessary military resources to occupy Moesia. Emperor Domitian realized he had to act quickly to counter Duras' offensive, travelling to Moesia at the head of a large military force and moving three legions to the territory of the menaced province. When the Roman army arrived, however, the Dacians avoided any direct confrontation with these superior forces. The war continued for several months, but without any major change in the strategic situation. On one occasion the Romans were ambushed and defeated by the Dacians, but the Dacians also suffered several defeats. In AD 86/87, Duras decided to abdicate in favour of a younger Dacian war leader named Decebalus, who had been the main military commander of the Dacians from the beginning of the conflict with Rome and had shown great personal capabilities on several occasions. The new king soon understood that there was no point in continuing the war with Rome, at least for the moment, since the Roman garrison of Moesia was by now too strong to be defeated. As a result, after Emperor Domitian had already left the theatre of operations, a peace treaty was concluded between the Dacians and the Roman Empire. According to the treaty, Decebalus returned the many Roman prisoners who had been captured by the Dacians and promised not to attack Moesia in the future; in exchange, he obtained Roman military assistance to build new fortifications on the territory of his kingdom and an annual subsidy of 8 million sesterces.

Thanks to the fortifications that were built with the help of the Romans, Decebalus could complete the reunification of Dacia that had been initiated by his predecessor and transform it into a centralized state. With the large amounts of money sent every year by the Romans, he could enlarge and re-equip his army, transforming it into a very efficient fighting machine. Decebalus quickly proved to be an excellent king, not only from a military point of view but also economically and administratively. He started to exploit in a methodical way all the great mineral resources of his kingdom in order to produce large amounts of precious metals, and also reorganized the structure of his state in order to exert better control over the peripheral areas of Dacia, where the local tribes were all brought under his influence. Decebalus also ordered the creation of a fortified capital for his realm, known as Sarmizegetusa. This soon became the most important political and religious centre in Dacia; it was erected on top of a mountain, at an altitude of 1,200 metres, in the centre of the kingdom. Sarmizegetusa, thanks to its position and fortifications, was extremely easy

86 Armies of the Thracians and Dacians, 500 BC to AD 150

Light infantryman of the Bastarnae carrying javelins and rectangular shield. (*Photo and copyright by 'Ancient Thrace'*)

Warrior of the Bastarnae armed with spear and hexagonal shield. (*Photo and copyright by 'Ancient Thrace'*)

to defend. It was made up of six connected citadels and was part of a larger system of fortifications. Sarmizegetusa had already functioned as the capital of the Dacians during the reign of Burebista, but after his death it lost its special status. It was not fortified or enlarged until the rise of Decebalus. During the decade that followed the end of hostilities between Dacia and Rome, Decebalus transformed his kingdom into one of the most flourishing states of Antiquity. He controlled a large portion of European territory, corresponding to modern Romania, and could put in the field an impressive army of more than 200,000 excellently equipped warriors. The Romans soon saw that signing a peace treaty with the Dacians had been a mistake, especially because of the overly positive conditions offered to Decebalus. Sooner or later, Rome realized, the Dacians would attack Moesia again, and consequently the Empire had to be ready to react. The Romans had bad memories of their previous war against the Dacians: the defeat of Oppius Sabinus and the humiliation suffered by the legions had not been forgotten. Decebalus had been the main cause of that Roman failure, when he was still just a military commander with the name of Diurpaneus; he only

Warrior of the Bastarnae equipped with spear and hexagonal shield. (*Photo and copyright by 'Ancient Thrace'*)

The First War with Rome and the Rise of Decebalus   89

Warlord of the Bastarnae with seax dagger. (*Photo and copyright by 'Ancient Thrace'*)

received the new moniker of Decebalus (i.e. "the Brave") after defeating and killing Oppius Sabinus in what became known as the First Battle of Tapae.

In AD 97, Trajan became emperor in Rome and started to deal with the most important military issues of the state. He considered Dacia as a substantial threat to the stability of the Empire, since it was too large to be considered a normal client state of Rome. In AD 101, after obtaining the Senate's blessing, Trajan started military preparations for the invasion of Dacia. By conquering Dacia the Romans would stabilize once and for all the northern borders of the Empire on the Danube; in addition, they would obtain access to the vast natural resources of a region they had never fully explored. From a cultural point of view, Dacia was a kingdom located on the edges of the known Roman world: the Romans considered the Dacians one of the many barbarian peoples living on their frontiers. Trajan prepared his invasion with great attention and assembled a large army to conduct it. The Dacians also got ready for a clash of arms, under the intelligent guidance of Decebalus. The king made great efforts to conclude a military alliance with the Sarmatians, a nomadic people from the steppes of Central Asia who had gradually driven out the Scythians from the plains of southern Russia and Ukraine during the third century BC. Like their Scythian enemies, the Sarmatians spent most of their life on horseback, their armies comprising mounted archers equipped with composite bows, alongside heavy cataphract cavalry with full armour and armed with spears. As the Sarmatians started to move south they practically eliminated the Scythians, occupying all their territory and establishing themselves north of Dacia. Decebalus was able to conclude a strong alliance with these steppe warriors, and in particular with the powerful tribe of the Roxolani, who provided him with large contingents of top-quality cavalry.

Chapter 8

The Roman Conquest of Dacia

Trajan reached the Roman province of Moesia in the spring of AD 101. He was at the head of one of the largest military forces ever assembled in the long history of Rome, which thanks to Cassius Dio we know comprised fifteen legions, ten *vexillationes* (i.e. detachments) of legions and eighty-nine corps of auxiliaries. The legions were the *I Adiutrix, I Italica, I Minervia, II Adiutrix, II Traiana Fortis, III Flavia, V Macedonica, VII Claudia, X Gemina, XI Claudia Pia Fidelis, XIII Gemina, XIV Gemina Martia Victrix, XV Apollinaris, XXI Rapax* and *XXX Ulpia Victrix*. The *vexillationes* came from the following legions: *II Augusta, III Augusta, III Gallica, IV Scythica, VI Ferrata, VII Gemina, IX Hispana, XII Fulminata, XX Valeria Victrix* and *XXII Primigenia*. The corps of *auxilia* comprised twenty-one *alae* of cavalry, thirty-three *cohortes equitatae* (mixed infantry and cavalry), twenty-five cohortes *peditatae* (infantry) and ten *cohortes sagittariae* (archers). In total, Trajan could count on 75,000 legionaries and 55,000 auxiliaries, supplemented by another 20,000 *auxilia* soldiers who were transferred to Moesia specifically for this campaign (the other 55,000 were already stationed along the Danube before the outbreak of hostilities). The emperor also brought with him the Praetorian Guard, which was the elite of the Roman Army and comprised Trajan's mounted escort. The Roman invasion force was divided into two large columns, which crossed the Danube on two pontoon bridges that were built from the warships of the Roman river fleet. Trajan's plan of campaign was simple: he would cross southern Dacia as soon as possible, ravaging all the enemy settlements encountered along the way, in order to rapidly reach the Iron Gates, a narrow mountain pass located west of the Dacian capital. Capturing them was the only way to approach Sarmizegetusa and enter inside the main fortified system of the Dacians. During the opening phase of the campaign, Decebalus acted in a very intelligent manner, avoiding a direct confrontation with the Romans and employing scorched earth tactics. All food reserves in southern Dacia were moved north or destroyed before the Romans could capture them as the Dacians retreated towards the heart of their lands and obliged the Roman army to move across densely forested areas. The Romans knew very little of these interior regions and their supply lines became increasingly stretched, to the point of being dangerously exposed to Dacian incursions.

Warlord of the Bastarnae. (*Photo and copyright by "Ancient Thrace"*)

The Roman Conquest of Dacia   93

Warrior of the Bastarnae armed with a long war club. (*Photo and copyright by 'Ancient Thrace'*)

Trajan continued his advance very slowly in order to avoid possible ambushes and to consolidate his presence in Dacian territory. While moving north, the Romans built camps, roads and bridges: by doing so, they would still have been able to put up a strong resistance in southern Dacia in case of defeat. When the Romans reached the Iron Gates, Decebalus decided that the time had finally come to fight a decisive pitched battle. What became known as the Second Battle of Tapae was extremely hard-fought by both sides. Eventually, the Romans were able to repulse the Dacian assaults, but only after suffering severe losses. Decebalus also lost many warriors, but he had plenty of time and resources to replace them. Following the battle, the Dacians retreated behind the Iron Gates and inside their main fortified system. Meanwhile, the Romans built a massive winter camp close to the entrance to the mountain pass. During the early months of AD 102, with the Romans blocked outside the Iron Gates, Decebalus decided to make a move on another front to divert Trajan's attention. Together with his Roxolani allies, he attacked Moesia from the north at the head of a massive military force. The Roman garrison of Moesia had great difficulty in containing Decebalus' invasion, but with the arrival of substantial reinforcements sent by Trajan, their situation improved. The Dacians and Roxolani made the fatal mistake of separating their forces, which enabled the Romans to react more effectively. Both the Dacians and the Roxolani were defeated, obliging Decebalus to abandon his plans for the opening of a second front. Trajan subsequently resumed his offensive in Dacia, after having reorganized his army into three separate columns. These would attack the Dacian fortifications from three different directions, having as their final objective the conquest of Decebalus' capital.

The Romans, albeit with great difficulties, were able to capture several Dacian fortifications and started to encircle Sarmizegetusa. At this point, probably in order to gain some time to reorganize his defences, Decebalus sent emissaries to Trajan with offers of peace. The Romans responded by proposing harsh conditions, which could not be accepted by Decebalus. As a result, the military operations soon resumed. During the following weeks, the Romans besieged and siezed all the Dacian fortifications around Sarmizegetusa. The Dacian Army attacked the Roman troops while they were besieging the last stronghold, but their offensive was repulsed with heavy losses for the attackers. Consequently, the way to the Dacian capital was open for the Romans. Decebalus' army had been defeated in the open field and there were no fortifications left in Dacian hands. The Romans, however, were extremely tired from their exertions: they had suffered significant losses since the beginning of the war and were by now very far from their own provinces. The siege of Sarmizegetusa would likely have lasted for several months, since the city was heavily fortified and built on top of a mountain; Trajan could not sustain a new campaign in a hostile land,

Warlord of the Bastarnae equipped with a short war club. (*Photo and copyright by 'Ancient Thrace'*)

Warrior of the Bastarnae armed with short war club and hexagonal shield. (*Photo and copyright by 'Ancient Thrace'*)

especially without sufficient supplies and fresh reinforcements. He therefore decided to terminate hostilities and conclude a peace treaty with Decebalus. The conditions imposed by the Romans to the Dacians were still very harsh: Decebalus had to accept the presence of several Roman garrisons on his territory and was forced to give up all the weapons of his army. In addition, he was asked to destroy all the fortifications of his realm and to cede part of his southern territories to the Roman Empire. Finally, the Dacians were required to accept Rome's protection and thus transform their kingdom into a client state of the Empire. Decebalus had no choice but to accept these humiliating conditions, in order to gain some time to prepare for a further clash with Rome. The military operations thus came to an end in AD 102, at least for the moment.

Soon after Trajan abandoned the theatre of operations with most of his troops, Decebalus reneged on the treaty and started preparing for a new war. He re-equipped his whole army with new weapons and rebuilt the fortifications around his capital that had been destroyed by the Romans. He attacked the Iazyges, a Sarmatian tribe that was allied with Rome, and ordered the execution of all those Dacian nobles who were in favour of respecting the Roman peace treaty. During June AD 105, following these events, Trajan responded by moving at the head of his forces towards Moesia again. When the Roman army arrived on the Danube, Trajan learned that his garrisons in Dacia had been massacred and that Decebalus was already waiting for him north of the river. Many Roman fortresses on the Danubian *limes* (i.e. border) had been attacked and occupied by the Dacians; as a result, Trajan had to spend the entire summer of AD 105 reconquering these fortified positions. During this early phase of the war, the Romans realized that it had been a mistake to not besiege Sarmizegetusa: it was clear by now that the only way to secure the Danubian frontier was to defeat Dacia and annex it to the Empire. Decebalus was too intelligent and too ambitious to be a vassal king, so it was essential to conclude the new conflict with his capture or execution. Knowing very well that conquering the whole of the Dacian Kingdom would be a difficult undertaking, Trajan remained south of the Danube until AD 106, reorganizing the defences of Moesia and assembling more military forces in anticipation of the upcoming invasion. During these crucial months of preparation, the Romans also completed the construction of a permanent bridge across the Danube. Thanks to this, the Roman army was able to move north and receive supplies and reinforcements much more easily than in the previous war. The Dacians were particularly impressed by the building of this bridge, which was incredible for the standards of the time, but they could do little to destroy it since it was defended by a substantial number of Roman troops. When it became clear that Trajan had crossed the Danube at the head of a massive invasion force, the main allies

Warrior of the Bastarnae with 'Suebian knot' hairstyle and war club. (*Photo and copyright by 'Ancient Thrace'*)

Warrior of the Bastarnae with long war club, which was burned to become harder. (*Photo and copyright by 'Ancient Thrace'*)

of Decebalus abandoned the Dacians to their fate: the Roxolani and the Bastarnae, who had made up a large proportion of Decebalus' forces during the previous conflict, had a change of mind and proclaimed their neutrality, thereby attempting to avoid the bloody vengeance of the Romans.

While these events took place north of the Danube, Trajan worked hard to receive military support from the Iazyges and the Germanic tribes that were settled on Dacia's north-western border. He wanted to be sure that these peoples would not collaborate with Decebalus, and further hoped that they could attack Dacia from another direction in order to open a second front against the Dacians. Seeing that Decebalus had been abandoned by his allies, the Romans launched their new invasion of Dacia. The Roman army was divided into two large columns: one would attack the fortifications of Sarmizegetusa from the west, forcing the Iron Gates, while the other would move from the east. The Roman advance was very difficult and slow, the Dacian warriors putting up strong resistance and defending their homeland to the last man. The fortifications rebuilt by Decebalus after AD 102, however, proved to be of inferior quality compared to those that had been constructed several years before with the assistance of Roman military engineers. As a result, they were swiftly overcome by the advancing Romans and their garrisons were either killed or captured. By the end of the summer of AD 106, all the Dacian fortified positions around Sarmizegetusa had been conquered and the two invading Roman columns joined forces. Trajan was now ready to besiege the Dacian capital with his vastly superior forces, but he had to act rapidly: winter was coming, and it would have been impossible for his soldiers to conduct a long siege against high ground in freezing temperatures. The emperor, however, was determined not to make the same mistake again: Sarmizegetusa had to be taken and Decebalus had to be neutralized at all costs. The siege of the Dacian capital, against all predictions, did not last long: the fighting between the defenders and the attackers was brutal, but the Dacians had lost most of their best warriors during the previous clashes and their population was exhausted. When the Roman soldiers entered the city, understanding that all was lost, many Dacian leaders committed suicide in order to avoid capture. Decebalus, however, did not consider the fall of his capital to be a mortal blow: he abandoned Sarmizegetusa before the end of the siege and moved north.

The Dacian king knew the territory of his realm intimately and had a clear idea how to continue the resistance against the invaders. He moved to the densely forested areas of the Carpathians, where he raised new forces and started planning another campaign, which had to be conducted using guerrilla tactics because the Romans were by now too numerous to be faced in pitched battle. The northern region of Dacia was the wildest of Decebalus' kingdom: it was far from the Danube and had few if any proper roads. Potentially, the Dacians could have resisted for years in the Carpathians; Decebalus hoped that a prolonged resistance would give him enough time to form new alliances with the Sarmatians and to raise more warriors. Trajan, after conquering Sarmizegetusa, formed a column of elite Roman troops and sent it north with orders to capture or kill Decebalus. The Dacian king no longer posed a danger to the stability of the Empire, since he commanded just a few retainers. However, if not neutralized, he could have resumed control over his kingdom at some point in the future by organizing a revolt of the Dacians against the Romans. The troops sent into northern Dacia had great difficulties in finding their enemy and had to advance very slowly: the local terrain was perfect for ambushes and they had no idea of its extent. The Dacians obtained some minor successes in this phase of the war, usually by attacking small Roman parties with hit-and-run tactics. Time was running out, however, and Decebalus had not yet been able to conclude another alliance with the Sarmatians. His military resources remained limited and the Romans were gradually conquering northern Dacia. Eventually, during one of the many skirmishes that took place in this final phase of the conflict, Decebalus and his retainers were located by a Roman cavalry unit made up of auxiliaries. Surrounded by enemy soldiers, the great Dacian king decided to commit suicide in order to avoid capture. All the other

Warrior of the Bastarnae with 'Suebian knot' hairstyle and war club. (*Photo and copyright by 'Ancient Thrace'*)

102   Armies of the Thracians and Dacians, 500 BC to AD 150

Warrior of the Bastarnae armed with short war club and hexagonal shield. (*Photo and copyright by 'Ancient Thrace'*)

leaders who were with him did the same, and thus the Romans captured only a few Dacians. The head of Decebalus was brought to Trajan a few days later.

With the death of the Dacian king, the war came to an end. The Romans continued to fight for some months more in Dacia, but only to put down minor local revolts. By the end of AD 106, the former Dacian Kingdom had been transformed into a Roman province, and the Empire now included a large portion of territory north of the Danube. The fall of the Dacian Kingdom, however, did not mark the end of the Dacians as an independent people. Many of them abandoned their homes after the Roman conquest and moved north in search of new lands, where they could live according to their traditions. These soon became known as the 'Free Dacians', in order to be distinguished from the majority of the Dacians who remained in their homeland under Roman rule. The Free Dacians settled on territories that were already inhabited by peoples of Dacian stock and where the presence of the Sarmatians was quite significant. These areas are today part of south-western Ukraine, Moldova and Bessarabia (a region of Romania). The two main communities of Dacian stock that already inhabited this region were the Costoboci and the Carpi. The Costoboci lived between the Carpathians and the Dniestr River, whereas the Carpi were located between the Siret River and the Prut River. From an ethnic point of view they were Dacians, but they had never been included in the Dacian Kingdom. Over the decades they had been strongly influenced by the culture of the Sarmatians, and thus were quite different from the ordinary Dacians. The Costoboci and the Carpi soon absorbed the refugees from the Dacian Kingdom into their own communities, and thus became part of the Free Dacians. After these events, the Free Dacians started to launch frequent raids against Roman Dacia, never accepting the loss of their homeland and always hoping that the Romans would abandon it. They were encouraged in their hope by the fact that the northern borders of Dacia were particularly difficult to defend for the Romans: there was no great river like the Danube to use as a natural barrier, and the frontier was too long to be defended with the construction of a wall.

The incursions of the Free Dacians started around AD 120, but were never perceived as a real threat by the Romans because they were merely lightning raids conducted by limited numbers of warriors. Over time, however, the Roman defences on their northern frontiers came under pressure. The Germanic tribes initiated their migrations towards the Roman Empire, and thus attacked the western part of the Danubian *limes*. Most of the Roman Army had to be deployed in that sector of the northern border, and thus the military presence in Dacia was reduced. The Dacians took advantage of this changing situation and attacked Roman Dacia several times between AD 120 and 275. They also started to no longer limit themselves to rapid incursions, but organized proper invasions of their ancient homeland. Several

Warrior of the Bastarnae equipped with short war club and small oval shield. (*Photo and copyright by 'Ancient Thrace'*)

The Roman Conquest of Dacia 105

Light infantryman of the Bastarnae carrying javelins and rectangular shield. (*Photo and copyright by 'Ancient Thrace'*)

emperors had to fight against the Free Dacians over two centuries: Antoninus Pius in AD 157, Maximinus I in AD 238, Decius in AD 250, Gallienus in AD 257, Aurelian in AD 272 and Constantine the Great in AD 337. On many occasions the Free Dacians were supported in their attacks by other peoples that were at war with Rome, such as the Sarmatians. The Romans were forced to garrison Dacia with large military forces until AD 275, in order to contain the incursions of the Free Dacians. The province always contained at least two legions and forty auxiliary corps, a total of around 35,000 soldiers. On many occasions these were barely sufficient to save Dacia from devastating raids. In AD 275, Emperor Aurelian decided to evacuate Dacia, considering it impossible to defend. At that time the Roman Empire was already under attack along all its borders, and there were insufficient resources to face all the menaces at once. Dacia was greatly exposed to foreign attacks and needed too many troops to be defended. As a result, the Romans abandoned the province and moved south of the Danube, where they established the new *limes*. All the Roman inhabitants of Dacia migrated to Moesia, and thus the local population could regain its independence. After several centuries of battles and hardships, the Free Dacians had finally achieved their objective. Constantine the Great briefly reoccupied part of Dacia in AD 337, but his successors were obliged to evacuate it again – this time forever. Unfortunately for the Dacians, their new-found independence did not last long, as just a few years later they were wiped out by the Goths who invaded Eastern Europe.

During the period AD 120–180, before the incursions of the Free Dacians into Roman Dacia became more significant, the Romans faced deadly attacks from the Sarmatians and their new Germanic allies, the Marcomanni. This was one of the bloodiest conflicts ever fought by the Roman Empire and, according to several scholars, marked the beginning of Rome's military decline. The so-called *Bellum Germanicum et Sarmaticum* (i.e. German and Sarmatian War) included several heavy defeats for the Romans, who had to employ all their resources to stop the migrations of the Germanic tribes on the Danubian frontier. Since the closing phase of Augustus' reign, the Romans had understood that conquering Germany was an impossible task for them and that they had to adopt a defensive attitude along the border region in northern Europe, which largely corresponded to the Rhine. This worked well until the age of Trajan, when the Empire reached its maximum territorial expansion, with the Germanic tribes easily contained by the *limes* and the Roman forces garrisoning it. When Marcus Aurelius became emperor, however, this situation started to change very rapidly: the Roman Empire was shattered by the outbreak of a terrible epidemic known as the 'Antonine Plague', that arrived in Europe from the Parthian territories in the Middle East, probably having been transported by the legionaries serving in Mesopotamia. The plague killed around seven million people and seriously

Duel between warriors of the Scordisci (left) and the Bastarnae (right). (*Photo and copyright by 'Ancient Thrace'*)

Assorted Germanic weapons of the Bastarnae. (*Photo and copyright by 'Ancient Thrace'*)

damaged the economy of the Empire. While these events took place in the Empire, the so-called 'Great Migrations' of the Germanic tribes started in Central Europe. The Goths began moving from their homeland at the mouth of the River Vistula, being under pressure from the steppe peoples of Central Asia. This migration of the Goths forced the Germanic tribes living along the borders of the Roman Empire, which had recently been quiet until then, to start moving west towards the Rhine and south towards the Danube. The first Germanic incursions across the *limes*, from AD 162–165, were easily repulsed by Roman armies, but these were just the beginning of a much bigger process. This became apparent when the Germanic Vandals and Sarmatian Iazyges invaded Dacia, killing its governor and devastating its territory. Meanwhile, the Marcomanni had crossed the Danube and attacked the Roman province of Pannonia (present-day Hungary) from the north.

Marcus Aurelius initially decided to concentrate his efforts in Dacia against the Sarmatians, recognizing that the province was particularly exposed to invasion. In the west, however, the situation became particularly serious when the Marcomanni and their warlord Ballomar were able to organize a confederation of tribes with the clear intention of conquering Pannonia. In AD 170, at the bloody Battle of Carnutum, some 20,000 Roman soldiers were defeated by Ballomar's warriors. After this clash, the Romans were expelled from Pannonia and the Germanic tribesmen continued their advance towards Noricum (present-day Austria) and northern Italy. This was the first time that foreign invaders had attacked the Italian peninsula since 101 BC, when the Cimbri and Teutones had raided north-western Italy. After these events, which had a great symbolic impact, Marcus Aurelius decided to concentrate all his military forces against the Marcomanni in Italy. By the end of AD 171, thanks to great efforts by the Romans, the Germanic warriors had been expelled from northern Italy and Marcus Aurelius was ready to launch a punitive expedition north of the Danube. Although the ensuing Germanic campaign of AD 172 was a success for the Romans, it did not destroy the great military potential of the Marcomanni. In AD 173–174, the Romans obtained a clear success over the Quadi, another Germanic tribe and the main ally of the Marcomanni. Consequently, the Romans could focus on defending Dacia and Moesia from the Iazyges, who had not yet been defeated. A new *Expeditio Sarmatica* (i.e. Sarmatian Expedition) was organized, which ended in AD 175 with a great victory for the Romans. The Sarmatians were forced to return all the Roman prisoners they had captured in the previous campaigns (some 100,000 individuals) and were obliged to provide 8,000 mounted auxiliaries to the Roman Army. These cavalrymen, equipped in the traditional Sarmatian manner, were sent to Britannia by the Roman authorities and remained there to protect the northern borders from incursions by the Celtic tribes settled in Scotland.

Points of Germanic spear and javelins. (*Photo and copyright by 'Ancient Thrace'*)

During the military events described above, the Free Dacians always sided with the Iazyges and participated in all the incursions directed against the Roman province of Dacia. By AD 175, however, both the Sarmatians and the Marcomanni had been temporarily defeated by the Romans and it seemed that Marcus Aurelius was on the verge of annexing their territories to the Empire (there were plans to create two new provinces, Marcomannia and Sarmatia). However, an internal rebellion prevented the emperor from securing his possession of the new lands that had been occupied north of the Danube. In AD 177, the Marcomanni and the Quadi rose up in revolt against Rome, having never truly accepted becoming 'clients' of the Empire. The Quadi were crushed after a savage campaign that was conducted in present-day Slovakia, and by AD 180 they no longer represented a threat to Rome, but in that year Marcus Aurelius died. This was a terrible blow for the Roman Army, since Marcus Aurelius' successor, Commodus, did not have the same strategic vision as his father and was not interested at all in military matters. Without strong leadership, the Roman troops were unable to effectively defend the frontiers. Commodus hastily concluded a peace treaty with the Marcomanni, so the problems of the northern *limes* remained unresolved. Meanwhile, the Free Dacians and the Sarmatians also rebelled against Rome and resumed their attacks on Dacia. Although the Romans were able to obtain a victory in that sector of the Danubian frontier in AD 182, it was not a decisive one. After Marcus Aurelius' death, the borders of the Roman Empire never again experienced a long period of peace: the Marcomannic Wars had shown the military weakness of the Empire, which was no longer in any condition to protect the long *limes*. The Marcomanni and Quadi were then joined by other Germanic tribes from the eastern regions of Europe, and these, by exerting strong pressure on Rome's territories, would eventually caused the fall of the Roman Empire. The role played by the Free Dacians during the Marcomannic Wars has never been fully considered, but it is important to bear in mind that they were different from the other peoples fighting against Rome: in contrast to the Germanic tribes and the Sarmatians, they had been expelled from their original homeland and were only struggling against the Romans to reconquer their former territories. The Marcomanni and Sarmatians, on the other hand, were in search of new lands to settle and wanted to invade the Roman Empire as a result of the mass migrations that were taking place in the eastern part of Europe.

Chapter 9

Thracian Military Organization and Tactics

Thracian military forces were organized along tribal lines, and thus each contingent was commanded by the war leader of the respective tribe. Each Thracian community had its own king or prince, who usually had strong military capabilities and extensive combat experience. Generally speaking, when fighting alone, single tribes could field armies of some 10,000 warriors. These were not paid for their military services, but were allowed to live on booty during campaigns conducted in enemy territory. Except for some small bodies of professional soldiers who formed the bodyguards of the kings/princes, no standing military units existed in times of peace. Each warrior had to pay for his weapons and personal equipment, since no central administration covered such organizational aspects. The Thracian forces mostly consisted of light infantry, but also included significant cavalry contingents. The standard Thracian light infantryman was the peltast, a skirmisher equipped with a crescent-shaped wicker shield (the *pelte*, from which he took his name) and a couple of throwing javelins. These fighters were able to move very rapidly and were perfectly suited for operating on broken terrain. As mentioned in previous chapters, most Thracian territory was covered by mountains and hills, where it was impossible to deploy troops in close formations like that of the Greek phalanx. Thracian warriors were used to fighting as skirmishers, and their wars were mostly inter-tribal conflicts which featured the raiding of bordering villages and cattle rustling. They wore no armour, and their javelins were perfect for their hit-and-run guerrilla tactics as they could be used to kill their enemies from a distance, for example during ambushes. The *pelte* was crescent-shaped in order to make the throwing of javelins more easy. Each peltast could throw a javelin from the top of the convex part of the shield, while protecting his torso behind the concave portion. Instead of a helmet, Thracian peltasts wore a cap made of fox-skin, perfectly suited to the cold temperatures of the Thracian winters thanks to the presence of a pair of earflaps. A square cloak and a long tunic, both very thick, were also worn. The traditional Thracian dress was completed by a pair of fur-lined fawn-skin boots, which were perfect to run on snow-covered terrain. The fur lining fell in three lappets, which was distinctively Thracian. Initially, the Greek hoplites had great difficulties in fighting the Thracians, since they moved too slowly to respond effectively to the rapid attacks of their opponents. As a result, some Greek commanders started to develop a

Germanic daggers of the seax type and small knife. (*Photo and copyright by 'Ancient Thrace'*)

new category of 'lighter' hoplites known as *ekdromoi*. However, such troops proved unable to face such a rapid enemy as the Thracians, so the Greeks also had to introduce peltasts into their own armies. In the beginning this was done by simply increasingly recruiting Thracian mercenaries, large numbers of which were always available. Yet as time progressed, the Greek cities started to train and equip some of their own citizen-soldiers as peltasts rather than as hoplites. Basically, in the Greek military system, a peltast was a sort of 'medium' infantryman: he did not have helmet or armour, but did carry a shield (unlike the regular light infantry of the javelineers and slingers). The Greek peltasts did not have the same traditional dress as their Thracian rivals, but did use their same basic equipment, with *pelte* shield and javelins. Heavy infantry was completely absent from Thracian armies. Consequently, so as to have some contingents of troops capable of fighting in close order, the Thracian leaders had no option but to recruit mercenary hoplites from Greece. It is important to note, however, that Thracian infantry did not comprise only peltasts: there were also light infantrymen armed only with javelins (without *pelte* shield), as well as archers and slingers. Infantry were much more numerous in the armies of the Thracian tribes which lived on hilly terrain, while the armies of tribes settled on level terrain had more cavalry. A standard Thracian army usually comprised 25 per cent cavalry and 75 per cent infantry, but some tribes (most notably the Odrysians) were able to deploy up to a 40 per cent cavalry.

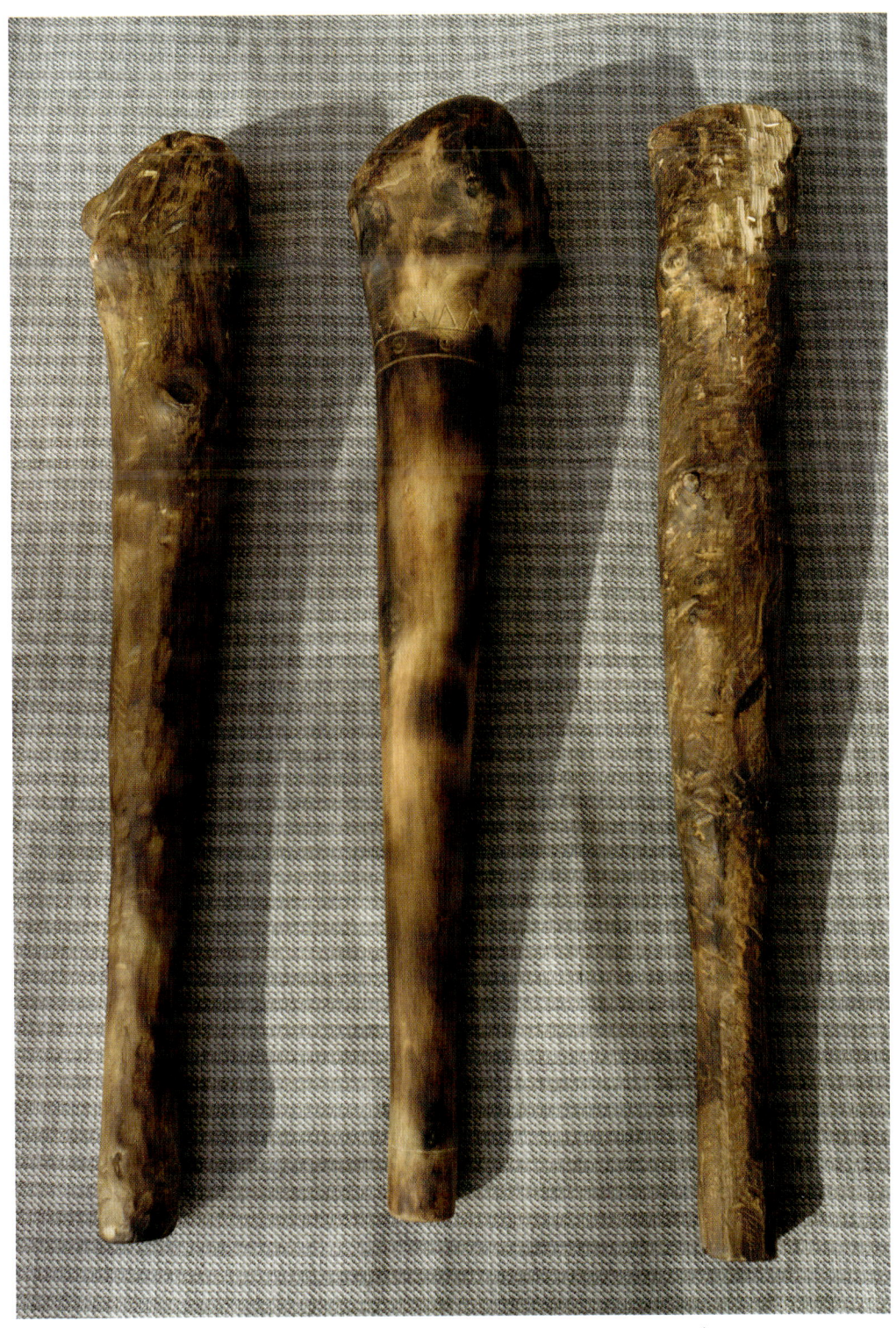

Germanic war clubs. (*Photo and copyright by 'Ancient Thrace'*)

Thracian cavalry was mostly made up of unarmoured, lightly armed horsemen equipped with a sword and two javelins. Sometimes a *pelte* shield could also be carried, strapped to the back of the cavalrymen for protection against attacks from the rear. There were also some small contingents of heavy cavalry equipped with helmet and armour: these made up the mounted bodyguards of the tribal kings and princes and could sometimes have small round shields for additional protection. Kotys, the greatest monarch in the history of the Odrysian Kingdom, had a large mounted bodyguard comprising 1,000 heavy cavalry. The Thracians were considered a race of natural horsemen by many ancient writers, and their mounts were of excellent quality; this was particularly true of the Getae, who had developed peculiar cavalry tactics due to their long contacts with the Scythae. The majority of the Getae cavalry were equipped as mounted archers and were armed with composite bows exactly like the Scythian horsemen. Some heavy cavalry also existed among the Getae, with scale armour and heavy spears like the cataphracts of the Scythians. The standard Thracian cavalryman was a sort of mounted peltast, since he was able to dismount very rapidly and act as a foot skirmisher if needed. The typical Thracian boots could be used while riding but also when moving on foot, being practical and comfortable to wear. Thracian horses were bigger than the ponies usually employed by steppe peoples and could be compared with the breeds of the Greek mainland. In times of peace they were trained for races, which were a popular sport practiced by several Thracian tribes. The Thracians were masters in producing horse trappings, which were highly decorated but effective. Until the ascendancy of Macedonia, all Thracian horsemen rode without saddles: this changed during the fourth century BC, when they came into universal use among the Thracians. The increasing success of Macedonian heavy cavalry convinced the Thracians to modify (at least partly) the equipment and tactics of their own cavalry. Most of the Thracian horsemen started to wear helmets for protection of the head and to carry shields for protection of the torso. Shields could be of three different kinds: round shields with a central boss, oval shields of *thureos* type or circular shields with a spine boss. The traditional short sword that had previously been carried was replaced by a longer version or by the *sica*, a peculiar Thracian weapon with a curved blade. All these changes took place during Lysimachus' long reign, when Thrace became part of the Hellenistic world. They were not adopted by the Getae, whose cavalry continued to be strongly influenced by that of the Scythians, for example, in using Scythian saddles.

As we have seen, Thracian infantry included other troop types in addition to peltasts, such as javelineers, archers and slingers. Javelinmen did not carry the *pelte* shield, and as a secondary weapon they usually had only a curved knife. Their javelins were different from those used by the peltasts, being lighter and shorter. Differently

Germanic hexagonal shield of the Bastarnae. (*Photo and copyright by 'Ancient Thrace'*)

Dacian warlord with full personal equipment. (*Photo and copyright by 'Historia Renascita'*)

from the peltasts, who usually had just two heavier and longer javelins, the javelineers carried a large bundle of throwing weapons. Archers were more common in the tribal armies of northern Thrace, rarely being used in the southern regions. The Getae infantry, for example, comprised significant numbers of archers, who were all equipped with the same composite bow as the Scythians. Slingers were recruited from the poorest herdsmen or shepherds living in mountainous areas, who were unable to equip themselves with the peltast panoply because of their economic condition. They were not common to find in Thracian armies, except when the raiding operations included the storming of hill forts. During the third century BC, Thracian light infantry started to be retrained in order to operate in close contact with the cavalry: this tactical change was already taking place in the Hellenistic world and was aimed at creating mixed forces of cavalry and light infantry. The foot skirmishers were now required to hamstring the enemy horses and support their own cavalry during close combat. By the early second century BC, most of the Thracian elite heavy cavalry contingents had attached corps of light infantrymen for combat support.

As mentioned in previous chapters, the Thracians served as mercenaries in several Hellenistic armies. The army of Lysimachus could not be considered as a 'Thracian' one, since the Macedonian general was never able to raise substantial numbers of Thracian warriors. His initial forces were mostly made up of Macedonian soldiers and Greek mercenaries, who constituted the garrison of Thrace during the final years of Alexander the Great's reign. After assuming effective control over his realm, however, Lysimachus was able to greatly increase the numerical consistency of his armed forces: by 301 BC, he had an army of 44,000 infantry and 3,000 cavalry. Lysimachus generally always preferred to avoid using the tribal contingents of the Thracians, so as not to cause the outbreak of revolts. Since he could not count on consistent numbers of Macedonian soldiers-settlers like the other Hellenistic monarchs, he mostly relied on mercenaries: these were frequently Illyrians, but also Greeks from the colonies located on the Thracian coastline. Over time, however, the master of Thrace also started to enlist an increasing number of Thracian tribal warriors: their status was that of allies and not of subjects, since the majority of them came from northern Thrace. Apparently, a certain number of these Thracians were trained and equipped in the Macedonian fashion in order to be employed as phalangists. After defeating Antigonus Monophtalmus, Lysimachus added Anatolia to his personal possessions, as a result of which he was able to start recruiting local contingents of Asian troops (mostly light infantry). After Lysimachus' death, these military forces passed under the command of Ptolemy Keraunos, who soon had to face a massive and destructive invasion of Celts. After being abandoned by the Thracians, the usurper was crushed with his remaining forces by the invaders.

118   Armies of the Thracians and Dacians, 500 BC to AD 150

Dacian warlord with helmet and scale armour. (*Photo and copyright by Historia Renascita*')

Dacian heavy infantryman with full personal equipment. (*Photo and copyright by 'Historia Renascita'*)

Macedonian armies of the Hellenistic period usually comprised several thousands of Thracian warriors: these, either mercenaries or allies, were mostly equipped as light infantry but sometimes could also serve as cavalry. Generally speaking, the Antigonid monarchs of Macedonia always tried to preserve as much as possible their precious Macedonian soldiers, preferring to employ mercenaries to perform dangerous tasks or secondary duties like garrisoning fortresses or cities. The Egyptian Army of the Hellenistic period included a good number of light cavalrymen, who were organized into four regiments (*hipparchiai*), each having a different ethnic composition: the first was made up of Thessalians, the second of Thracians, the third of Mysians and the last of Persians. These horsemen were all military settlers, who arrived in Egypt as mercenaries and remained in the realm as colonists, living in the area of the Nile delta. By the second century BC, however, the four *hipparchiai* of light cavalry were no longer named after their original ethnic composition. Thracians were also employed as mercenaries in the Egyptian Army: at the Battle of Raphia (217 BC), for example, there were a total of 6,000 Thracians fighting for Egypt, 4,000 of whom were military settlers and the remaining 2,000 newly recruited mercenaries. Minor numbers of Thracian mercenaries, either light infantrymen or light cavalrymen, were also present in the Seleucid Army. The Pontic Army of Mithridates VI was always a very multinational military force, since the ambitious king tried to develop a unified cultural identity among the different peoples living in the Black Sea region, with the objective of uniting them against Rome. For this reason, he could count on the support of numerous mercenaries and allies: Greeks, Thracians, Galatians, Scythians and Sarmatians. The Thracians were not extremely numerous and fought in their usual manner as light skirmishers. The Greek colonies of Crimea, which temporarily came under the political influence of Pontus, also frequently contracted contingents of Thracian mercenaries. Under Herod the Great, the military forces of the Kingdom of Judea included a large Royal Guard that comprised around 2,000 men: these were Idumaeans, Thracians, Galatians and Germans. The latter three groups were made up of mercenaries, while the Idumaeans were recruited from Herod's most loyal subjects. Each of the four ethnic groups forming the Royal Guard was organized into an independent unit of 500 soldiers. Apparently, all the bodyguards of Herod were able to serve both as infantry and cavalry.

Thracian tactics were very difficult to deal with for their opponents, especially when the tribal warriors were operating on their home territory. On several occasions, as we have seen in the previous chapters, the Thracians managed to organize successful ambushes against large invading forces that were crossing their lands. Long columns, especially if slowed by the presence of carts transporting supplies, were an easy target for the javelins of Thracian skirmishers. Apparently, the Thracians were also able to

Dacian heavy infantryman with helmet and chainmail. (*Photo and copyright by 'Historia Renascita'*)

Dacian heavy infantryman armed with spear and oval shield. (*Photo and copyright by 'Historia Renascita'*)

launch cavalry charges downhill, thanks to the good training of their horses: as a result, during these ambushes they could also employ their horsemen effectively. Generally speaking, the Thracians preferred to avoid pitched battles, especially against the Greeks, since they had no heavy infantry and thus had no chance of countering the enemy phalanxes. When forced to fight in the open field, they developed their peltasts in open order and attacked the enemy from a distance, trying to cause as many casualties as possible without closing to hand-to-hand combat with their opponents. These tactics were also employed by the Thracian cavalry, who, at least initially, were not able to sustain a long fight against heavy cavalrymen such as those of the Macedonians. The heavy and long javelins used by the peltasts were so effective that they could easily kill an armoured hoplite, even if the latter protected himself with a shield. When charged by a phalanx, the Thracians usually retreated very rapidly but continued to harass their opponents by throwing their javelins. They thus caused many losses to the enemy without being engaged in a close-range fight. When forced by circumstances to face the enemy in close combat, the peltasts were usually massacred by the heavier infantrymen: their *pelte* shields were designed for protection against enemy javelins and thus could do little against the spears or swords of the hoplites. Not all battles, however, were fought on the ideal plain terrain that was perfect for phalanx formations: sometimes an important clash could take place on hilly terrain, where the hoplites experienced serious problems. Initially, the Greeks had little or no light troops in their armies, and thus could not secure victories over the Thracian tribes that they faced. Over time, however, they started to recognize the great potential of light infantry and introduced peltasts into their military system.

This led to some important changes in Thracian tactics, since the flanks of the Greek phalanxes were no longer vulnerable to their surprise attacks. During this same period, the Greeks also started to expand their cavalry contingents, which meant that more fast moving troops were now available to counter the Thracians. Peltasts could easily be crushed by enemy cavalry if charged on open terrain, since they could not deploy themselves in close order like the hoplites with their long spears. As a result of the innovations introduced by the Greeks, Thracian tactics started to change too. Thracian cavalry regularly began to employ shields, and helmets also became much more popular. Consequently, the mounted peltasts were able to fight against Hellenistic heavy cavalry much more effectively, albeit continuing to be armed with javelins on most occasions. The standard equipment of the foot peltasts was also made heavier, in order to transform them into medium infantry. This had already happened in the Greek world, where the peltasts had assumed various new tactical functions that were different from those of the hoplites but also from those of the 'proper' light infantry equipped only with light javelins or slings. The tactical innovations introduced by the Thracians during the Hellenistic period were mostly the result of foreign influences: by fighting against Hellenistic armies or by serving as mercenaries within them, the warriors of Thrace learned how to modify their traditional combat style. During the whole period here taken into account, the Getae remained different from the other Thracians, since they never came under strong Hellenistic influence but continued to be equipped like the Scythians living on their northern borders. Getae heavy cavalry, consisting of cataphracts, used wedge formations to charge the enemy, whereas Getae light cavalry employed composite bows exactly like those of the steppe peoples living in Central Asia. The Danube was at this time essentially a frontier between two worlds: to the south of it, Greek and later Hellenistic military models were dominant; to the north, the tactics of the Scythians were the most common.

Chapter 10

Thracian Military Equipment

The standard national uniform of Thracian warriors comprised the following four basic elements: a tunic, a cloak (*zeira*), a cap (*alopekis*) and a pair of boots (*embades*). The tunic and cloak were produced in bright colours, the latter being a distinctive feature of Thracian dress; they were usually decorated with geometrical patterns, which could be very intricate. Obviously the quality of the tunic and cloak varied according to the economic position of each individual warrior. According to ancient sources, Thracian tunics and cloaks were renowned for their excellent texture, being made of hemp, flax or wool. Some differences existed between the uniforms worn by the northern Thracians and those used by fighters living in the south. In the north of Thrace, narrow trousers and a short shirt were added to the tunic and cloak to provide better protection from the cold *temperatures*. During winter months, especially in mountainous regions, a fur cloak was usually worn over the standard *zeira*. Tunics were fastened with leather or textile belts, which could be richly decorated with metal elements. The 'national' Thracian cap could be produced in three main versions. The first was obtained from a fox's skin and had the face of the animal perched above the wearer's forehead, with flaps of patterned cloth on the neck and on the cheeks. The second cap was low-crowned and was made of cloth or felt, while the third was high-crowned and had the classical shape of what later became known as the 'Phrygian cap', which was produced in one piece, including the flaps covering the neck and cheeks. According to ancient sources, the first version was the most popular, since the fox was a sacred animal in the traditional religion of the Thracians. Among the tribes of northern Thrace, wearing the *alopekis* was a mark of social distinction and only the nobles were permitted to do so: most of the ordinary warriors therefore had no cap. The Getae did not wear the traditional Thracian costume described above, instead being dressed more or less like the Scythians. They wore jackets with coloured edges, long-sleeved shirts, trousers and pointed boots, an outfit clearly designed for cavalry use. Caps, if worn, were of the same kind used by the Scythians. The basic Thracian tunic was knee-length and sleeveless, being tied around the waist by a belt, with a boss that could be heavily decorated. The cloak covered the whole body, but without hampering movement. It was made from heavy material and thus was quite stiff. The standard Thracian cloak reached the ankles and

126 Armies of the Thracians and Dacians, 500 BC to AD 150

Dacian heavy infantryman equipped with spear and oval shield. (*Photo and copyright by 'Historia Renascita'*)

Dacian warrior with full heavy equipment. (*Photo and copyright by 'Historia Renascita'*)

was perfect for protecting the body from cold temperatures during the winter. Its top portion could be folded over and its top corners turned in to hang over the chest or be thrown back over the shoulders. The cloak was held in place by a single brooch, fixed on the left shoulder. The traditional Thracian boots, the *embades*, were manufactured from fawn-skin and covered the lower part of the leg as well as the whole foot. They were laced at the front, with some flaps (usually three) hanging down from the top. These boots were ideal for running over rocky terrain, even if covered with snow, and were worn also by Thracian cavalrymen.

With the beginning of the Hellenistic period, especially after Alexander the Great's death, the general appearance of Thracian warriors started to change as Greek cultural influence spread across Thrace. Until that time, Thracian warriors had decorated their bodies with extensive tattoos and had worn very long beards: by the middle of the fourth century BC these could no longer be found, together with some items of dress that had always been peculiar of the Thracians. Cloaks, boots and caps were gradually abandoned, being replaced by the usual Greek style of dress that was in the process of being exported across the Hellenistic world by the Macedonians. Tunics assumed the standard Greek cut and were no longer decorated with the typical Thracian patterns. Consequently, most Thracian warriors became practically indistinguishable from their Macedonian and Greek equivalents (except for their weaponry). The new tunics could have long or short sleeves, and were usually produced in dark colours. The Celtic invasion that caused the fall of Ptolemy Keraunos also left some traces of its passage across Thrace, with Thracian warriors starting to wear the traditional torcs of the Celts around their necks.

At the time of their first contacts with the Greeks, helmets and armour were not very common to find in the panoply of Thracian warriors. Only the nobles and their heavy cavalrymen used personal protections made of metal, and most of the fighters only carried the *pelte* shield for defensive purposes. This general situation changed only during the fourth century BC, when an increasing number of peltasts started to have helmets and greaves. The introduction of these elements can be seen as a consequence of the peltast's gradual transformation from light to medium infantryman. Thracian helmets and armour had always been practically identical to those used in mainland Greece, the only exception to this rule being the Getae of northern Thrace, who used the same panoply as the Scythians. It is interesting to note that some models of helmets or armour, which were obsolete by Greek standards, continued to be employed in Thrace for a long time. It seems that the Thracians were quite slow in adopting the equipment innovations introduced in Greece. For geographical reasons, the warriors from southern Thrace usually had the most updated panoplies. Mixtures of helmets and armour from different styles were not uncommon, since Thracian armies did not have the same uniformity as their Greek or Macedonian equivalents. Complete defensive equipment was used only by a few rich individuals: the majority of the Thracian warriors usually had just one or two pieces of armour, even after the partial Hellenization of their country. In the later period of Thracian military history, when Macedonia was transformed into a Roman province, the previous Hellenistic influence started to be replaced by the new Roman one. The bodyguards of the Thracian client kings started to use Roman helmets and chainmail, thus completely abandoning their national military traditions.

Dacian warrior with helmet and chainmail. (*Photo and copyright by 'Historia Renascita'*)

Dacian warrior carrying a spear and hatchet. (*Photo and copyright by 'Historia Renascita'*)

The Thracian warriors used four different models of Greek helmets: Corinthian, Chalcidian, Attic and Phrygian/Thracian. The Corinthian helmet was introduced during the last phase of the Greek Dark Ages and remained the most popular model of helmet during most of the early Classical Period, right until the outbreak of the Peloponnesian War in 431 BC. As is clear from its name, it was probably designed for the first time in Corinth, but it should be remembered that it was part of the Greek 'archaic panoply' discovered at Argos that also comprised the famous Argive shield and the 'bell cuirass'. The Corinthian helmet included a frontal plate that covered the entire face, thus providing excellent protection to the wearer. As time progressed, however, the need for better visibility and reduced weight led to the eventual abandonment of this model of helmet, which was substituted by new ones open on the face. The Corinthian helmet only had three thin slits in the plate protecting the face: two for the eyes and a vertical one for the mouth/nose. On the back, a large curved projection protected the nape of the neck. When not fighting, a Greek hoplite would wear his Corinthian helmet tipped upward for comfort, although this practice was not common among the Thracians. One of the main characteristics of the Corinthian helmet was the presence of an indentation in the bottom edge dividing the jawline from the neckline, but over time this was replaced by a simple dart. The greatest fault of the early Corinthian helmets was that they made hearing practically impossible, so the surface of the helmet located on the ears started to be gradually cut away. Before adopting this solution, several experiments were made, which led to the creation of a new helmet that derived directly from the Corinthian one: the Chalcidian helmet. The Chalcidian helmet was probably designed for the first time in Chalcis, and thus was extremely popular among the Greek hoplites from the large island of Euboea. It was lighter and less bulky than a Corinthian helmet, since it left the entire face and ears of the wearer completely free, having no frontal plate. As a result, hearing and vision were much better compared to a Corinthian helmet. The Chalcidian helmet consisted of a hemispherical dome under which there were a pair of cheek pieces and a neck guard, while on the front there was a very small nasal bar. The cheek pieces could be fixed or hinged to the helmet. Adornments or protuberances of various kinds could be attached to the top of the helmet's dome. Various experiments were made to improve the Chalcidian helmet, leading to the introduction of a new model known as the Attic helmet. As is clear from its name, this was widely used in the region of Attica and thus in Athens. It was one of the latest models of helmet to be developed during the Classical Period and was also in widespread use during the subsequent Hellenistic Period. In general terms, the Attic helmet was quite similar to the Chalcidian one, but did not have the latter's nose guard. Cheek pieces were hinged and not fixed, as in the later examples of Chalcidian helmet. The Attic helmet could be decorated in

Dacian warrior with sleeveless chainmail. (*Photo and copyright by 'Historia Renascita'*)

Thracian Military Equipment 133

Dacian warrior armed with a curved knife. (*Photo and copyright by 'Historia Renascita'*)

a variety of ways: these included incisions, adornments and protuberances of various kinds that were sculpted or applied on its external surface. As we have seen, the Corinthian, Chalcidian and Attic helmets were all linked together and were part of a common evolutionary process that started during the Dark Ages of Greece. The Phrygian/Thracian helmet, however, started to be produced after the Greeks came in close contact with the warriors inhabiting Thrace and Phrygia. Basically, it was a metal version of the Phrygian cap that was worn by many of the Thracian and Phrygian fighters. It had the same apex as the Phrygian cap and was characterized by the presence of a peak at the front, which shaded the wearer's eyes and offered some additional protection. Sometimes, instead of the peak, a Phrygian/Thracian helmet could have a small nasal bar similar to the one on Chalcidian helmets. A couple of large cheek pieces were attached to the main body of the helmet; frequently these were enough large to form a full facial mask, having only three small gaps for the eyes and nose/mouth. All the helmets described above were usually decorated with crests of horse hair, attached with props, pins, hooks or rings. The Getae warriors used conical Scythian helmets, which had eyes and eyebrows embossed and gilded on the forehead; usually these were richly decorated with figures of animals and had a high-domed skull. Curiously, the hig dome was the result of the Getae's practice of using the same hairstyle as the Scythians that prescribed the wearing of a top-knot. Scythian helmets also had rectangular cheek-guards, a short neck-guard and cut-outs in the areas of the ears and face. Decorations were richly detailed on the helmets of nobles, but were quite simple on those of common warriors.

Until the fourth century BC, Thracian armour followed Greek patterns quite closely. At the beginning of the period here taken into account, the standard armour worn by Thracian nobles was that commonly known as 'bell cuirass' (because of its shape) or 'Argive cuirass' (because its oldest example has been discovered in Argos). This kind of armour derived from the previous models employed during the late Mycenean Period and was introduced on a large scale during the closing phase of the Greek Dark Ages. It consisted of a front and a back plate made of bronze, simply decorated in the form of the anatomy of the torso: this decoration was very basic and consisted just of a few lines. The two plates were linked together by two tubular projections that were fitted into corresponding slots and held in position with two pins, but also with two loops placed at the bottom of the left side (one on the front plate and one on the back plate). The plates were held in position on the shoulders with two iron spikes placed on the front plate, which passed through corresponding holes on the back plate. In addition, under the left arm and at the left hip, the rolled-over edge was opened up to form a channel that held the front plate of the cuirass in position. Around the neck, arm holes and bottom edge of the cuirass there were embossed

Thracian Military Equipment   135

Dacian elite warrior with *draco* standard and scale armour. (*Photo and copyright by 'Historia Renascita'*)

Dacian elite warrior with *draco* standard and scale corselet. (*Photo and copyright by 'Historia Renascita'*)

ridges obtained by rolling forward the bronze. The overall shape of the cuirass resembled that of a bell, being much larger in the bottom half. The Argive cuirass was usually worn together with several additional components, which made it quite heavy but extremely complete: a semi-circular plate known as a *mitra*, suspended from a waistbelt worn under the cuirass and protecting the abdomen; shoulder guards; arm guards (usually for the right arm only); thigh guards; greaves; ankle guards; and foot guards. All these additional protections were made of bronze and could be decorated with incisions in the same fashion as the cuirass. These elements derived from the Mycenean panoply employed centuries before in Greece, and made the warriors using them look to be encased in bronze. As time progressed, all these additional defensive elements fell into disuse, except for the greaves, although they could be found in Thrace well after they had become outdated around Greece.

During the period from 550–500 BC, the bell cuirass declined in popularity and was rapidly substituted with the new 'muscle cuirass', the external surface of which was sculpted with great detail in order to reproduce perfectly the anatomy of the torso. The new model of cuirass could be quite short, reaching the waist, or long enough to cover the abdomen. The new muscle cuirass also consisted of two separate bronze plates, joined together at the sides and at the shoulders with hinges (one half of the hinge was attached to the front plate and the other half to the back plate). Usually there were six hinges on each cuirass: two on each side and one for each shoulder. On either side of each hinge there was a ring that was used to pull the two plates of the cuirass together. Generally speaking, the muscle cuirass was worn on a very large scale during the period of the Persian Wars, but by 450 BC it was no longer the most common model. The Greeks started to feel the need for an increased level of mobility that could not be achieved while wearing heavy bronze cuirasses, which were also quite difficult and expensive to produce. As a result, by the outbreak of the Peloponnesian War, linen had become the standard material for producing corselets. To replace the uncomfortable *mitra*, by the time of the Persian Wars the Greeks had already started to employ linen or leather in order to produce the so-called pteruges: these were strips/lappets that were assembled to form a sort of defensive skirt that could be worn under the bronze cuirass. Since they were extremely effective, especially against enemy arrows, the pteruges quickly became popular and also started to be employed to protect the shoulders and upper arms, being worn under the muscle cuirass on the shoulders. The linen cuirass (i.e. a cuirass entirely made of linen) was already used during the Persian Wars and had the great advantage of being particularly light and easy to wear. It consisted of multiple layers of linen pressed and glued together in order to form a corselet about 0.5cm thick. This corselet extended down to the hips, and its lower part, below the waist, had slits in order to make it easy to bend forward.

Dacian warrior blowing his horn. (*Photo and copyright by 'Historia Renascita'*)

Dacian warlord armed with dagger and knife. (*Photo and copyright by 'Historia Renascita'*)

These slits formed a line of pteruges, which were part of the main cuirass rather than a separate component. Under the main corselet, another layer was worn which also had pteruges but was stuck on the inside of the cuirass in a way that made it cover the gaps opened in the pteruges of the outer layer. The whole corselet was produced as a single-piece object and thus was wrapped around the torso before being tied together on the left side. A specifically designed U-shaped plate, always made of linen, was worn on the shoulders; this was fixed to the back of the corselet and pulled forward to protect the frontal part of the shoulders. Soon after the appearance of the linen cuirass, the Greeks produced an updated version of it that was known as the composite cuirass: basically, this was a standard linen cuirass that was reinforced by adding bronze scales on its external surface. These scales were usually assembled in a large band placed around the waist, but they could also be placed on other points of the corselet, such as the shoulders or the loins. Sometimes a linen corselet could be entirely covered with bronze scales, but these costly examples of composite cuirass were quite rare. By the end of the Peloponnesian War, most of the Greek hoplites fought without armour, but only with helmet and shield. However, this general trend was not exported to Thrace, where the noble warriors continued to wear muscle or linen cuirasses for a long time, until well after Alexander the Great's death. Greaves also continued to be used in Thrace, albeit on a small scale; these could be decorated in many different ways, for example reproducing the anatomy of the lower leg or with geometric incisions. They could be pulled open and clipped on to the leg or strapped at the back.

The Scythian armour used by the Getae heavy cavalry was made up of bronze or iron scales fastened with bronze rings to a leather backing, which could be applied on the leggings too in order to protect the legs from enemy arrows. Scale armour was very flexible and thus easy to wear on horseback. Corselets of this kind could have long or short sleeves, and on many occasions they could also have attached pteruges, covered with scales like the rest of the armour. Collars/pectorals obtained from a single piece of metal were frequently worn over the corselets of Scythian armour.

As secondary weapons, the Thracian warriors employed swords and knives. These, however, were not particularly popular because the Thracians were not used to hand-to-hand fighting. Swords were of the same models used by the Greeks: the *kopis* and the *xiphos*. The *kopis* was a heavy cutting sword with a forward-curving blade, the latter being single-edged. One-handed, it had a blade length of 48–65cm, which pitched forward towards the point and was concave on the part located nearest to the hilt. The peculiar recurved shape of the *kopis* made it capable of delivering a blow with the same power as an axe. A peculiar version of the *kopis* was the *machaira*: this had all the same features, but its blade was not recurved. The *kopis* was particularly

Dacian warrior equipped with a *falx*. (*Photo and copyright by 'Historia Renascita'*)

Dacian tribal warrior armed with a *falx*. (*Photo and copyright by 'Historia Renascita'*)

appreciated as a cavalry weapon, due to the peculiar shape of its blade; the *machaira*, instead, was primarily an infantry sword. The *xiphos* was a one-handed, double-edged short sword with a straight blade, the latter measuring between 45 and 60cm. It usually had a midrib and was diamond or lenticular in cross-section. The *xiphos* had a quite long point and thus was an excellent thrusting weapon, specifically designed for close combat. Initially, among the Thracians, swords were carried only by noble warriors who were rich enough to also have some kind of armour; with the partial Hellenization of Thracian armies, however, they became much more common. Generally speaking, the *kopis* was much more widely used before the military ascendancy of Macedonia, while the *xiphos* was introduced on a large scale during the Hellenistic period. Judging from surviving examples, Thracian swords had the same main features as their Greek equivalents, from which they were copied, but had longer blades. This distinctive characteristic gradually disappeared when the *xiphos* became the most common model of sword. All Thracian warriors were equipped with a simple knife with a curved blade, which could be a deadly weapon when used during close combat. The Getae did not employ the *kopis* or the *xiphos*, but a Scythian model of sword that was also used in the Persian Empire: the *akinakes*. This was carried in a distinctive scabbard that had a large side piece, or 'ear', for attachment, which allowed the sword to hang at an angle to its belt. The scabbard was made of wood covered with leather, and was designed for use on horseback. The pommel of the *akinakes* consisted of two narrow strips of iron rising and curling inwards. Later models of this sword had a simpler pommel with an oval shape. The grip, originally cylindrical, later became double-tapered in order to be easier to hold. In addition to swords and knives, the Thracians had another deadly weapon in their national panoply, the *rhomphaia*. This was a two-handed cutting weapon similar to a sickle, and had a long blade which could be straight or slightly curved and was single-edged. The *rhomphaia* was almost entirely made of iron, having just a wooden or bone grip covering the tang of the handle. The blade had an overall length of 50–60cm, and thus was particularly impressive. The *rhomphaia* was perfect to hamstring horses, which made it an excellent anti-cavalry weapon; in addition, it could easily sever a head from its body. During the Hellenistic period, when the Thracian peltasts gradually transformed themselves into medium infantry, an increasing number of them started to substitute javelins with a *rhomphaia*. This was quite heavy to transport, so only the strongest warriors were usually equipped with it. It was particularly feared as a weapon for hand-to-hand fighting, as it could easily kill an armoured soldier with just a single blow. The *rhomphaia* was also quite popular among the Bastarnae, who were usually equipped with this sickle and two javelins.

144   Armies of the Thracians and Dacians, 500 BC to AD 150

Dacian tribal warrior equipped with *falx*. (*Photo and copyright by 'Historia Renascita'*)

Dacian warrior armed with composite bow. (*Photo and copyright by 'Historia Renascita'*)

As we have seen, the basic equipment of a Thracian peltast always comprised a *pelte* shield and two 'twin' javelins. The *pelte*, which did not have a rim or any kind of metal facing, was made of wicker or wood and was covered with goatskin or sheepskin. The Thracian shield was usually carried with an arm strap and a handle at the rim, but it could also be transported on the back, being slung thanks to a back strap. On the back of the shield there was a simple central grip. Generally speaking, the *pelte* was key for the tactical success of the peltasts: thanks to this small but versatile shield, the Thracian warriors had a great advantage over the enemy light infantry who did not carry any form of body protection. It was light to transport and could also be employed by horsemen. It was designed for a fighter who had to throw javelins and was perfectly suited to protect its user from enemy arrows.

Thracian javelins had a very simple blade made of metal and were long, between 1 metre and 1.5 metres. They were heavier and longer than the usual javelins carried by the traditional Greek light infantry, and thus each Thracian warrior carried just a couple of them. According to ancient sources, the Thracians were masters in using their throwing weapons: they could hit the enemy from long distances and with incredible accuracy. This was obviously the result of daily training and constant exercise. Until the third century BC, not all Thracian peltasts were armed with a couple of javelins; some of them were equipped with a spear that was 3 metres in length. This spear was obviously designed for close combat and not as a throwing weapon. The presence of some warriors armed with a spear was an important element of Thracian tactics, especially when clashes with the Greeks became frequent. Those fighters armed with spears acted as a screen for their companions throwing javelins. In case of enemy counter-attack or of defeat, the warriors equipped with spears would protect the retreat of the peltasts, who were particularly vulnerable after throwing both their javelins. Spearmen were not organized into separate groups, but a certain number of them were usually mixed among the standard peltasts. They were of great use when the peltasts were charged by enemy cavalry or when a formation of hoplites came too close to the javelin-armed warriors.

At the beginning of the fourth century BC, Iphicrates, thanks to the tactical lessons learned while fighting in Thrace, completely reformed the Athenian Army by changing the standard panoply of the hoplites and peltasts. Iphicrates' reforms, which were absolutely revolutionary for the time, did not save the Athenian Army from its slow decline, but did have a fundamental impact over the development of the new Macedonian phalanx introduced by Philip II. From a tactical point of view, the new Macedonian phalangist was just an improved version of the lesser-known Iphicratean hoplite. Iphicrates was the first to see the great potential of the peltasts as a sort of medium infantry, which could fight both as light skirmishers and as heavy shock

Dacian warrior equipped with composite bow. (*Photo and copyright by 'Historia Renascita'*)

148　Armies of the Thracians and Dacians, 500 BC to AD 150

Dacian archer with composite bow. (*Photo and copyright by 'Historia Renascita'*)

troops according to circumstances. In 391 BC, at the Battle of Lechaeum, Iphicrates was able to defeat a contingent of Spartan hoplites with just a force of peltasts, the first time in history this had happened. During previous years, he had already modified the panoply and tactics of the Athenian peltasts: instead of the traditional *pelte* shield, Iphicrates gave them a large oval shield (always made of wicker); in addition, the new peltasts wore a helmet for protection against head injuries. Offensive weapons now also included a short sword and a short spear, in addition to the usual javelins. Thanks to the larger shield and new helmet, the Iphicratean peltast could fight in close combat against a hoplite, while the new sword and spear gave him more or less the same offensive capabilities as a heavy infantryman. Compared to a hoplite, however, the new peltast was much more mobile since he wore no armour. In practice, Iphicrates had completed the transition of the peltast from a light to a medium infantryman. After the positive experience of Lechaeum, the Athenian general also decided to modify the panoply and tactics of the standard hoplite. The large hoplon shield was abandoned in favour of a much smaller and lighter round shield; the metal greaves were discarded and replaced by new leather boots known as Iphicratids, from the name of their creator, which were very similar to the Thracian ones; new lighter cuirasses made of quilted linen replaced the older models; and the spear, to compensate for the lightening of the defensive equipment, was lengthened up to 3.6 metres. The new small shield could be strapped to the forearm, thus freeing the left hand to help holding the new longer model of spear. To sum up, Iphicrates made the panoply of the peltasts heavier and that of the hoplites lighter. As stated previously, Philip II adopted the equipment prescribed by the Athenian general for the new hoplites as the standard panoply of his Macedonian phalangists. The Iphicratean reforms were not adopted in other cities of Greece, while even in Athens they never had a universal diffusion; if they had been, the Greeks may well have been able to face the expanding Macedonian Army on equal terms and with more chances of victory.

It is important to note, however, that by 250 BC most of the Hellenistic states – including some of the Thracian tribes – had completely re-equipped their own peltasts. The Celtic invasions had obliged the Hellenistic armies to face a new kind of enemy: the Celtic warrior, having the offensive weapons of a light infantryman but at the same time carrying a large defensive shield. The Hellenistic commanders, influenced by their new enemies, soon copied the Celtic personal equipment and created a new category of soldiers known as *thureophoroi*. Basically, a *thureophoros* was a type of medium infantryman, a new version of the traditional Thracian-type peltast; his name derived from the *thureos* shield, which was a Greek copy of the usual Celtic oval shield, with metal strip boss and central spine. Each *thureophoros* also carried a sword, a long thrusting spear and two javelins; armour was not used, but each soldier had a helmet. Apparently the Celtic oval shield had already been adopted by some Illyrians and Thracians before the Greeks, so most of the mercenary and allied infantrymen sent to Macedonia by these peoples during the wars against Rome were already a sort of *thureophoroi*. In general terms, the *thureophoros* operated in an intermediate role between the heavy infantry phalangist and the light infantry skirmisher. They could support the light infantry thanks to their large shields, but could also deploy themselves in phalanx formation thanks to their thrusting spears. Apparently this new category of soldiers was perfectly suited to the military needs of the smaller Hellenistic states: thanks to their great mobility over every kind of terrain, the *thureophoroi* were frequently used as border troops. Their tactical flexibility and adaptability were much appreciated by the Greek cities, with the result that most of the Greek hoplites or peltasts soon started to be re-equipped with the oval *thureos*. Since the days of Philip II and Alexander the Great, it had been clear to Macedonian military commanders that the most significant weakness of the phalanx was its exposed flanks: this problem became particularly apparent when the Hellenistic armies started to face the Roman legions. After the first defeats caused by the tactical superiority of the legions, the commanders of the various Hellenistic armies started to reform their troops in order to create a new category of soldier that could protect the flanks of the phalanx and fight against the Roman legionaries on almost equal terms. To achieve this ambitious objective, they started to transform the *thureophoroi* into a Hellenistic version of the legionaries. These new soldiers were soon known as *thorakitai* – which means 'cuirassed soldiers' – because they were equipped with chainmail armour exactly like their Roman opponents. In general, we could say that the *thorakitai* were *thureophoroi* with armour: the addition of chainmail transformed them into heavy infantrymen, who carried the same kind of oval shield used by the Romans, who had copied it from the Celts like the *thureophoroi*. Deployed on the flanks of the phalanx, the *thorakitai* were flexible and well-equipped enough to confront the Roman legionaries either in skirmish order or in hand-to-hand combat. Unfortunately for the Hellenistic states, however, the reform of the *thorakitai* remained quite limited from a numerical point of view and could not change the course of the wars fought against Rome.

Chapter 11

Dacian Military Organization and Tactics

From a cultural point of view, the Dacians were quite different from the Thracians: across the centuries, they had developed a sedentary way of life in which agriculture played a prominent role. Most of the Dacians were free farmers, who lived on several acres of fertile land and had a good number of domestic animals. Their agricultural production was abundant enough to provide food for the whole year to their families, and thus each Dacian community was completely autonomous from an economic point of view. From the days of Burebista's reign, the Dacians also started to extract large amounts of natural resources from the numerous mines of their homeland. This enabled them to become richer and to improve their general conditions of life. When the various tribes of Dacia were unified under Decebalus' rule, their way of life changed quite significantly: the central state started to exert some form of control over agricultural production and several public constructions were built on the territory. Decebalus ruled over Dacia as an absolute monarch, but with the fundamental support of the country's aristocracy. The aristocracy was particularly powerful, since nobles were the only members of society capable of raising warriors in case of conflict; as a result, they could greatly influence the military and foreign policy of the king. Generally speaking, the Dacian farmers were excellent warriors. They were used to harsh living conditions and knew how to employ their weapons in the most effective way. The infantry were the main component of the Dacian military forces, since cavalry consisted of just a few mounted skirmishers with light equipment. Under Decebalus, however, the Dacian Kingdom was able to conclude an alliance with the Roxolani (Sarmatians), who provided the Dacians with large and excellent cavalry contingents. These used the equipment and tactics that were typical of the steppe peoples: they could be heavily armoured cataphracts or lightly equipped mounted archers. During their first war against Trajan, the Dacians were also supported by large numbers of foot soldiers provided by the Bastarnae and Scordisci, ferocious fighters who were particularly feared by the Romans because of their great combat skill. Consequently, we could say that the Dacian Army – especially under Burebista and Decebalus – was a multi-national force, comprising Dacian infantry and cavalry, Sarmatian cavalry, Bastarnae infantry and Scordisci infantry. The basic Dacian infantryman was different from the

152 Armies of the Thracians and Dacians, 500 BC to AD 150

Germanic warrior of the Goths, who were allies of the 'Free Dacians'. (*Photo and copyright by 'Ancient Thrace'*)

Full heavy panoply of a Dacian warlord. (*Photo and copyright by 'Historia Renascita'*)

Thracian peltast: he was armed with throwing javelins but carried a large shield, and was armed with a sword with a straight blade. Most of the Dacian warriors did not wear armour, except for the nobles, who usually also had helmets and mostly fought on horse. In addition to the light skirmishers mentioned above, the Dacian cavalry also included some small contingents of heavy horsemen provided by the aristocracy. These were known as *tarabostes*. Almost 75 per cent of the Dacian Army consisted of infantry armed with javelins or spears, the remaining part comprising small quotas of archers and the cavalry (divided between light horsemen and armoured nobles). Considering the standards of the Ancient World, the Dacian armies deployed by Burebista and Decebalus were impressive from a numerical point of view. With the support of their allies, the Dacians could easily deploy an army of 100,000 warriors against their enemies. Unlike the Thracians, the Dacians had no problems in fighting pitched battles and were equipped to face the Roman legions in close combat. Since the days of Burebista's wars against the Celts of Transylvania, the Dacians had adopted the large oval shields used by the Celts, and this enabled them to fight against any kind of heavy infantry. The Dacian warriors, however, always retained a high degree of mobility, since they never used armour on a large scale. Like the Thracians, no permanent military units existed in peacetime except for the small bodyguards of the king and the major nobles. In times of war, the warriors were assembled on the battlefield according to their tribal origins and were commanded by the nobles of their respective community. They were not paid for their military services and did not receive their personal equipment from the administration of the state. When operating on enemy terrain, however, they were permitted to pillage and raid unrestrictedly.

After the war with Domitian, in view of future conflicts with Rome, Decebalus decided to retrain part of his military forces according to contemporary Roman models. This was something that the Thracians had already done during the previous decades and that could have transformed the Dacian Army into a much more effective fighting force. Decebalus, in particular, was interested in improving the general quality of his infantry: he wanted to introduce the same close tactical formations as the legions, and to do this he needed Roman instructors. Initially he hired Roman deserters who had joined his cause or Roman prisoners of war who had been captured during the conflict with Domitian. Later, as a result of the peace conditions agreed with the Romans, he could count on the Roman military engineers who were sent to Dacia to rebuild the local fortifications. Apparently, however, Decebalus' programme of military reforms never became effective as the Romans in his service were too few to retrain the whole Dacian Army and the king had to face serious internal opposition that made the introduction of military innovations practically impossible. The Dacian nobles did not want to change their traditional way of fighting, and were against their warriors being equipped like the Roman legionaries. Since the tribal contingents of the Dacian Army were all controlled by the aristocracy, Decebalus had no choice but to renounce his plans. Generally speaking, the Dacian Army always suffered from the divisions emerging between the king and his aristocracy: no standing royal army existed, which greatly limited the personal power of Decebalus.

The allies of the Dacians, who were a fundamental component of their army, always retained their own military organization and tactics, which for the Bastarnae and Scordisci were clearly Celtic. At the beginning of a battle, Celtic infantry were deployed in great masses according to their own tribal/family provenance. Before charging the enemy, they used all their weapons of psychological warfare in order to spread terror in their opponents' ranks. First of all they slashed the air with their long swords and poured abuse on the enemy, producing a great noise with terrible war cries and by banging their weapons on their large shields. This incredible spectacle was completed by the tossing of standards and by the terrific braying of horns and trumpets. During this initial phase, some champions – chosen warriors – usually came out of their ranks and engaged in duels with the best fighters of the opposing army. The outcome of these single combats usually had a deep impact over the morale of the two armies deployed on the field, so were not merely a secondary part of a battle's

Dacian Military Organization and Tactics 155

Full panoply of a Dacian heavy infantryman. (*Photo and copyright by 'Historia Renascita'*)

Full equipment of a Dacian heavy infantryman. (*Photo and copyright by 'Historia Renascita'*)

early phase. After some time spent carrying out these preliminary activities, the Celtic warriors charged the enemy en masse, during which they continued to scream and to slash the air with their swords, hoping to cause a breaking of the opponent's line due to panic. Shortly before investing the first line of the enemy, Celtic warriors equipped with javelins – who were deployed in the first lines – used their missile weapons to break the integrity of the enemy formation. Once in direct contact with the enemy, each Celtic warrior engaged in a duel with an opponent, these individual clashes – which could last from a few seconds to several minutes – being decided by the physique and swordsmanship of the individual fighters. Generally speaking, Celtic tactics were extremely simple: if the frontal assault described above was repulsed, Celtic warriors had no alternative but to launch another similar one. These frontal charges would continue until the enemy army was broken or until the Celtic fighters became exhausted. Very frequently, after a failed assault, the Celts completely lost their morale and were crushed by an effective counter-attack mounted by their enemies. The chances of victory for a Celtic army were strongly related to the success of the first charge: if that failed, Celtic warriors generally lost their impetus and tended to abandon the battlefield. The infantry, however, was not the only component of Celtic armies. Light troops, both foot and mounted, had little tactical importance and were mostly employed to harass the enemy during the early phases of a combat or during guerrilla operations conducted on broken terrain. Heavy cavalry, on the other hand, played a major role in Celtic warfare. The majority of Celtic cavalrymen, being noble warriors, had heavy personal equipment, including helmet and chainmail; their offensive weapons included javelins (used during the first phase of a combat), spear and long slashing sword (employed during frontal charges).

The Sarmatian tribes had a military organization that was quite similar to that of the Dacians. Each community had its own tribal chief, who was a warlord with great experience and exerted control over the other nobles, who commanded the various contingents of warriors. Small permanent bodies of professional fighters did exist, but these usually acted only as the bodyguards of the aristocrats. The majority of the warriors were called to serve only in the event of war. Differently from what happened in the Dacian Army, they could receive part of their panoply from the noble under whom they were serving. Each man was a potential warrior, as the Sarmatians spent most of their life on horseback and were trained to use the bow since childhood. Sarmatian military forces consisted almost entirely of cavalry, with very small quotas of foot soldiers, who were mostly recruited from the subject peoples that they had defeated. Sarmatian cavalry featured a large number of horse archers armed with the composite bow and a smaller – but still significant – number of heavy cataphracts. These heavy cavalry were armed with a two-handed heavy spear

Decorated helmet of a Dacian warlord. (*Photo and copyright by 'Historia Renascita'*)

known as the contus, which could be used with devastating effects against any kind of enemy, either mounted or on foot; for this reason, they were considered to be the best of all Sarmatian warriors, and Decebalus always tried to have large numbers of them under his command. The horses of the cataphracts were armoured like their riders, and this made the Sarmatian heavy cavalry practically invulnerable to enemy arrows. Sarmatian cavalry tactics were based on feigned retreats, which were followed by rapid attacks that encircled the enemy and crushed it with a rain of arrows. When the enemy was subsequently concentrated in a single point of the battlefield, a final charge by the cataphracts usually concluded the battle in their favour.

Chapter 12

Dacian Military Equipment

The Dacian national uniform was quite simple, consisting of the following elements: long tunic, fringed cloak, loose trousers and leather footwear. The footwear was quite simple and did not consist of boots like with the Thracians but of simple shoes. Most of the foot warriors wore the traditional loose trousers typical of the Dacians, but 'normal' trousers similar to those worn by the Celts were also used. The tunics were decorated in a very simple way and, differently from those of the Thracians, they were not ornamented with complex geometrical patterns. The cloaks, which were mostly worn by the richest warriors, could have intricate decorations that sometimes resembled the tartan patterns of Celtic dress. After the Celts settled in Transylvania, the Dacians started to be influenced by their way of producing clothes and an increasing Celtic influence started to be seen in Dacian dress. The fringed cloaks were a mark of social distinction and were of especially great use during winter. Tunics were comfortable to wear, being split at the neck and at the sides, while trousers could be tied in at the ankle. The cloak was held in position by a metal brooch, which was on the left shoulder. The dimensions of the cloak varied according to the economic position of its wearer: ordinary warriors had shorter cloaks with simpler decorations, while noble warriors wore longer cloaks with more complex decorations. The social position of a Dacian warrior could also be understood by observing his headwear. Generally speaking, caps were worn only by the aristocrats, who had the privilege of covering their heads. Common warriors, however, sometimes wore simple skull caps. The standard headgear of the Dacian nobles was the Phrygian cap, which was generally smaller compared with that worn by the Thracians. This could be of different colours and was the most distinctive element of the Dacian national dress. During the summer, most of the warriors fought with bare chest, wearing no tunic. The tunic was usually made of wool, like the cloak, and thus was not practical to use during warmer months. Linen tunics and trousers, however, were also common to find. The tunics of noble warriors, be they made of wool or of linen, were usually decorated on the hem and on the cuffs. A simple waistbelt made of leather tended to be worn, to keep the trousers in the correct position.

The great majority of Dacian warriors did not have helmet or armour, the latter defensive elements being used only by the aristocrats. The most common model of

Various models of Dacian helmets. (*Photo and copyright by 'Historia Renascita'*)

helmet was the Phrygian/Thracian one, made of bronze and with no facial mask. This could be heavily decorated with incisions and had a vertical crest obtained from a single layer of bronze. This crest, typical of the Dacian version of the Phrygian/Thracian helmet, followed the profile of the helmet's top part, which had the shape of a classical Phrygian cap. Sometimes a neck-guard, created from bronze scales assembled together, was positioned on the back of the helmet for protection of the neck. Dacian armour was of the same kind employed by the Sarmatians, consisting of iron or bronze scales with a leaf shape. To produce a single corselet, hundreds of iron or bronze scales were needed. Dacian corselets were short-sleeved and were worn over tunics. This kind of armour, which was light to wear, was mostly designed to protect its wearer from enemy arrows; it was less effective when worn during close combat. Sometimes simple bronze greaves were worn by noble warriors. Generally speaking, however, only a very small percentage of the Dacian warriors had a helmet and corselet: the great majority of them, both on foot or mounted, had the shield as their only personal protection. Dacian shields were the same as those used by the Celts and had an oval shape. They were part of that category known as 'bodyshields', because they were long enough and large enough to protect a warrior from the shoulders to the ankles. Most of them had a central spine made of wood and a boss (*umbo*) made of metal, which was designed to reinforce the whole structure of

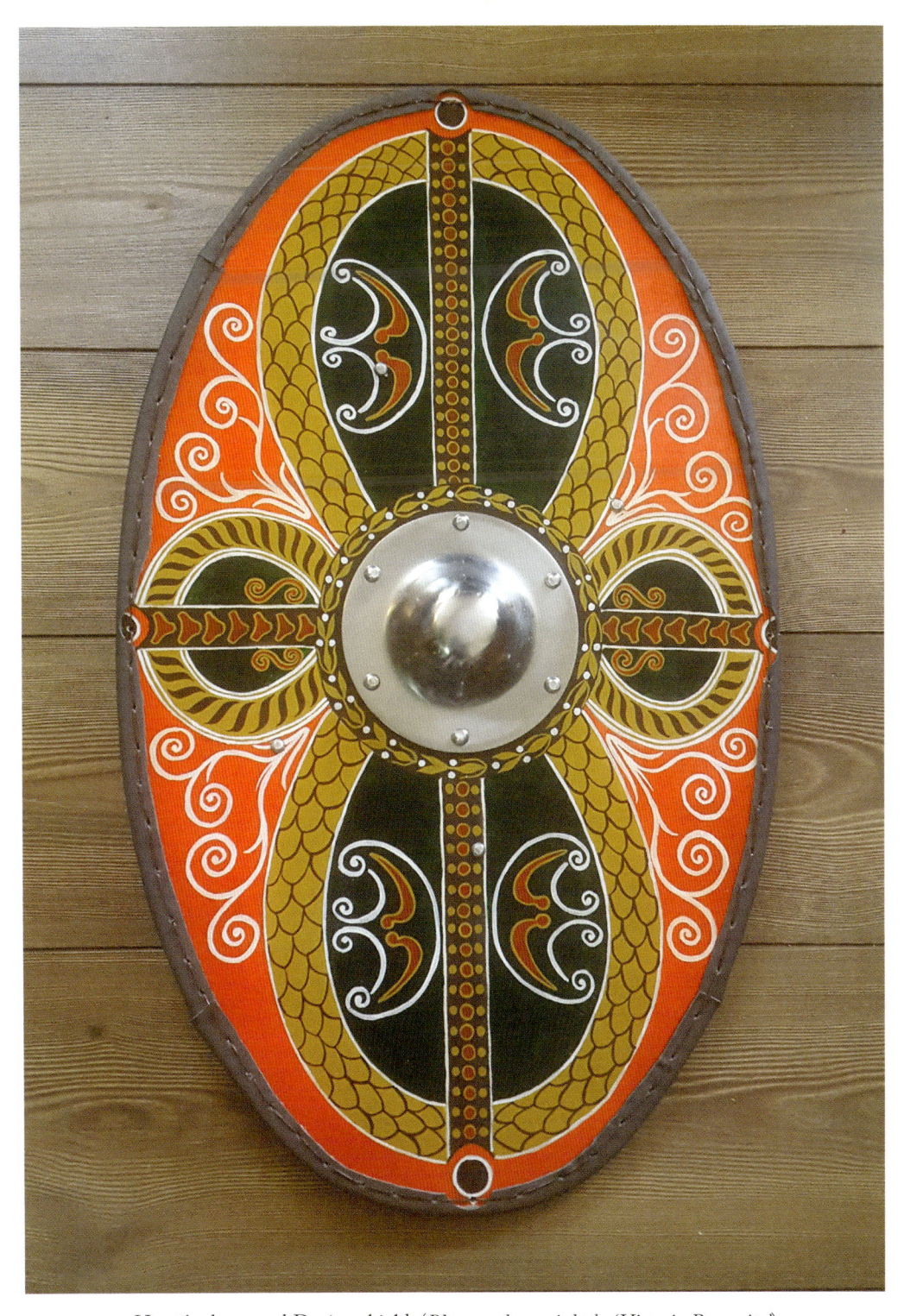

Heavily decorated Dacian shield. (*Photo and copyright by 'Historia Renascita'*)

Dacian oval shield. (*Photo and copyright by 'Historia Renascita'*)

Dacian shield painted with decorative patterns. (*Photo and copyright by 'Historia Renascita'*)

the shield. Bosses were oblong and could have different shapes. Dacian shields were made of oak planks, which were chamfered to a thinner section towards the rim; the wooden spine, swelling in the middle, was shaped in order to correspond with a round or oval cut-out in the shield centre. The strap-type metal boss crossed over the wider section of the spine and was riveted on the external surface of the shield. The surface, on both sides or only on the front, was entirely covered with leather, which could be painted in various bright colours and have decorations of several kinds (generally representing sacred animals or flowers/plants). Bosses corresponded to the handle of the shield on the back, and thus had a fundamental function in protecting the user's hand. Additional metal binding was frequently attached to the external edges of the shield, in order to reinforce it.

The offensive weapons of the Dacians comprised spear, javelins, sword, curved knife and *falx*. The spears had points entirely made of iron that could be of different shapes: the most common one had its edges curving inwards from the belly of the blade to its tip. An average Dacian spear was more or less 2.5 metres long. Most of the Dacian warriors did not have a spear but carried a couple of javelins, which were lighter than those employed by the Thracian peltasts and were designed for fast throwing. The long slashing swords of the Dacians were of the same kind as those used by the Celts, having been adopted after the first Celtic communities settled in Transylvania. The blade of these weapons had a distinct elongated leaf shape, being double-edged and having a square-kink or shallow 'V' point (the sides of which were drawn at an angle of 45 degrees to the axis of the blade). The tang of these swords – the internal part of the handle, made of metal but covered with organic material – swelled sharply, to a point of greatest width that was placed just below its centre. The ricasso – the unsharpened length of blade just above the handle of the sword – was very short and had a notch that varied greatly in depth. Sword handles were made of wood or leather and generally had the form of an 'X'. The handle was completed by a pommel, which was connected to the tang by way of a rivet-hole. The blade itself measured from about 60–90cm in length and was entirely made of iron or steel. The shape of the point clearly demonstrates that these weapons were used for slashing and not for thrusting. Generally, blades had a broad neck, with the greatest width being usually low down towards the point. Swords were transported in iron scabbards, which were sometimes richly decorated with incisions and/or bosses. The scabbards reproduced the general shape of the blade and were constructed from two plates: the front plate, slightly wider than the back one, was folded over the latter along the sides. Scabbards were generally suspended on the warrior's right hip from a sword belt made of leather. Dacian knives, like those of the Thracians, had a curved blade and were particularly effective when employed during hand-to-hand fighting.

Dacian Military Equipment 165

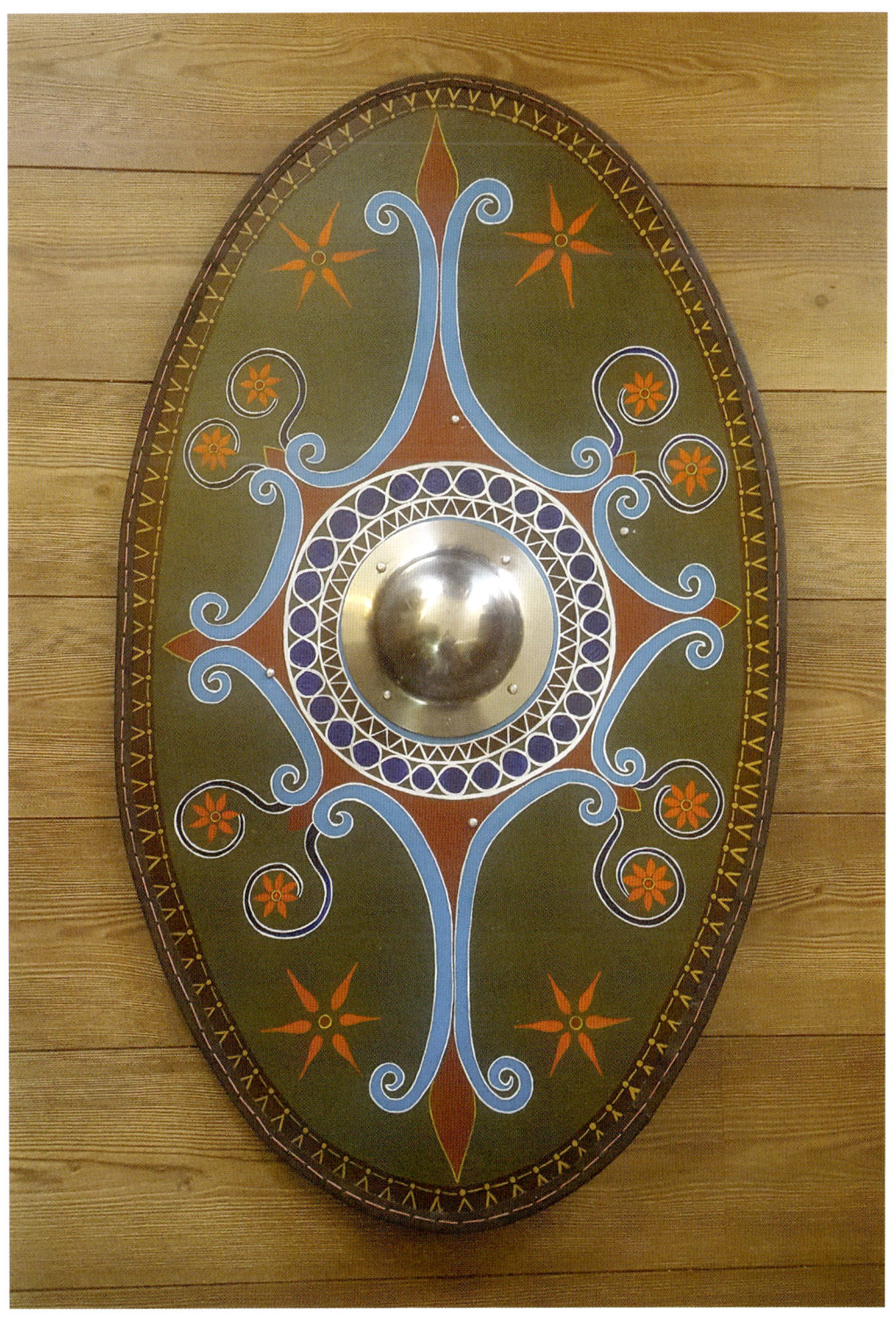

Decorated Dacian shield. (*Photo and copyright by 'Historia Renascita'*)

Dacian sword. (*Photo and copyright by 'Historia Renascita'*)

The *falx* was the deadliest component of the Dacians' offensive panoply and their truly 'national' weapon. It was a two-handed cutting weapon similar to a sickle and had a long blade, which could be straight or slightly curved and was single-edged. In practice, it was the Dacian equivalent of the Thracian *rhomphaia*. The *falx* was almost entirely made of iron, having just a wooden or bone grip covering the tang of the handle. The blade had an overall length of 50–60cm and thus was particularly impressive. It was perfect for hamstringing horses, and thus was an excellent anti-cavalry weapon; in addition, it could easily sever a head from its body. The *falx* was also produced in a shorter, single-handed version known as a *sica*: this was not very different from the standard knives with a curved blade but its bigger dimensions made it perfect to use in hand-to-hand fighting when confronting an enemy equipped with a short sword. The *falx* was too long to be used in a narrow space; in addition, it was two-handed and consequently the warriors employing it could not protect themselves with a shield. As a result, many of the Dacian warriors used the *sica* as an alternative to the sword, while those equipped with the *falx* operated as an elite force that was charged with breaking the enemy lines. The blade of the *falx* was sharpened only on its inside edge, and thus was designed to slash an enemy after having hooked him with the curved point. For this reason, the *falx* was perfect to destroy the shields of an enemy formation and could easily take off the arms or legs of an enemy from a certain distance. During Trajan's campaigns in Dacia, the Roman legionaries had serious problems in facing Decebalus' warriors because many of them were equipped with the *falx*. To protect their arms and legs during close combat, the Romans had no option but to wear additional armour made of metal over the most exposed parts of their bodies. Only the stronger Dacian warriors could use the *falx*, since a great deal of energy and training were needed to employ it in an effective manner. These fighters, in order to be completely free in their movements, usually wore no armour.

The Dacian national panoply also comprised another distinctive element, the *draco* standard. This had originally been created by the Sarmatians and was later adopted by the auxiliary cavalry units of the Roman Army. As is made clear by its name, it had the form of a dragon, with open wolf-like jaws containing several metal tongues. The hollow head of the dragon was made of metal and was mounted on a pole, with a long fabric tube fixed to the rear. When used, the *draco* was held up in the air, where it filled with air and made a shrill sound as the wind passed through its metal tongues. It was a perfect addition for psychological warfare, especially during the early phases of a pitched battle.

The few Dacian archers were usually armed with composite bows of the same kind used by the Sarmatians, but longbows entirely made of wood – similar to the Celtic versions – were also employed. Arrows were carried in quivers, that could be richly decorated.

168 Armies of the Thracians and Dacians, 500 BC to AD 150

Different models of Dacian swords. (*Photo and copyright by 'Historia Renascita'*)

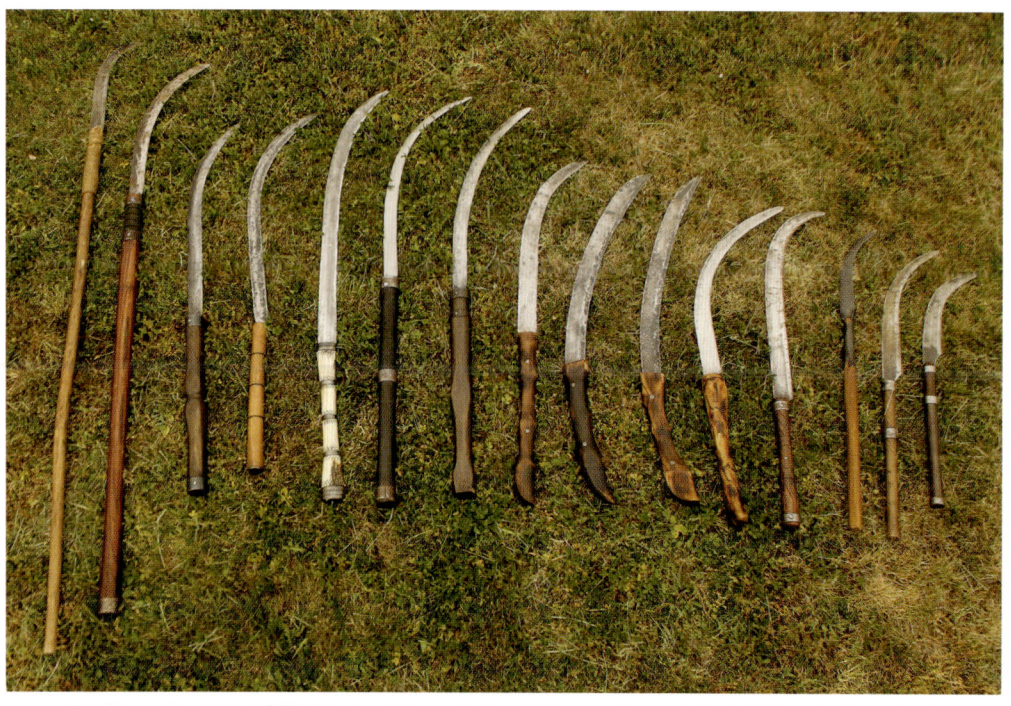

Different versions of the Dacian falx and sica. (*Photo and copyright by 'Historia Renascita'*)

Dacian Military Equipment 169

Some examples of Dacian *falx*, *sica* and curved knife. (*Photo and copyright by 'Historia Renascita'*)

Some examples of Dacian curved knives. (*Photo and copyright by 'Historia Renascita'*)

170 Armies of the Thracians and Dacians, 500 BC to AD 150

Dacian belts with decorated buckles. (*Photo and copyright by 'Historia Renascita'*)

Some examples of Dacian jewels. (*Photo and copyright by 'Historia Renascita'*)

Bibliography

Primary sources
Appian, *Roman History*
Arrian, *Anabasis of Alexander*
Diodorus Siculus, *History*
Dionysios of Halikarnassos, *Roman Antiquities*
Herodotus, *The Histories*
Livy, *History of Rome from its Foundation*
Plutarch, *Lives*
Polybius, *The Histories*
Quintus Curtius, *History of Alexander*
Strabo, *Geography*
Thucydides, *History of the Peloponnesian War*
Xenophon, *Anabasis*
Xenophon, *Hellenica*
Xenophon, *Kyropaidia*

Secondary sources
Anderson, E.B., *Cataphracts: Knights of the Ancient Eastern Empires* (Pen & Sword, 2016)
Baker, P., *Armies and Enemies of Imperial Rome* (Wargames Research Group, 1981)
Beazley, M., 'Thorakitai: armed after the Roman fashion', *Ancient Warfare Magazine*, volume X, issue 2
Brzezinski, R. and Mielczarek, M., *The Sarmatians 600 BC–AD 450* (Osprey Publishing, 2002)
Cernenko, E.V., *The Scythians 700–300 BC* (Osprey Publishing, 1983)
Connolly, P., *Greece and Rome at War* (Frontline Books, 1981)
Dean, S.E., 'Cataphracts: heavy cavalry of the Mithridatic Wars', *Ancient Warfare Magazine*, volume X, issue 3
Everson ,T., *Warfare in Ancient Greece: Arms and Armour from the Heroes of Homer to Alexander the Great* (The History Press, 2005)
Goldsworthy, A., *The Fall of the West: The Slow Death of the Roman Superpower* (Weidenfeld & Nicolson, 2009)
Gorelik, K., *Warriors of Eurasia* (Montvert Publishing, 1995)
Head, D., *Armies of the Macedonian and Punic Wars* (Wargames Research Group, 1982)
Macdowall, S. and McBride, A., *Germanic Warrior AD 236–568* (Osprey Publishing, 1996)
McDonnel-Staff, P., 'Hypaspists to Peltasts: the elite guard infantry of the Antigonid Macedonian Army', *Ancient Warfare Magazine*, volume V, issue 6
Post R., 'Bright colours and uniformity: Hellenistic military costume', *Ancient Warfare Magazine*, volume IV, issue 6

Quesada Sanz, F., *Armas de Grecia y Roma* (La Esfera, 2014)
Rocca, S., *The Army of Herod the Great* (Osprey Publishing, 2009)
Sekunda, N., *The Army of Alexander the Great* (Osprey Publishing, 1984)
Sekunda, N., *The Ancient Greeks* (Osprey Publishing, 1986)
Sekunda, N., *The Seleucid Army* (Montvert Publishing, 1994)
Sekunda, N., *The Ptolemaic Army* (Montvert Publishing, 1995)
Sekunda, N., *Macedonian Armies after Alexander 323–168 BC* (Osprey Publishing, 2012)
Warry, J., *Warfare in the Classical World* (Salamander Books, 1997)
Webber, C., 'Fighting on all sides: Thracian mercenaries of the Hellenistic Era', *Ancient Warfare Magazine*, volume IV, issue 6
Webber, C., *The Thracians 700 BC–AD 46* (Osprey Publishing, 2001)
Wilcox, P. and Embleton, G., *Rome's Enemies 1: Germanics and Dacians* (Osprey Publishing, 1982)

The Re-enactors who Contributed to this Book

Ancient Thrace

The living history association 'Ancient Thrace' was created in 2015 as a historical re-enactment group by enthusiasts from Yambol in Bulgaria, who were fascinated by the ancient history of their land and wanted to express their passion for it. By now the association has around twenty regular members and many friends from various places who often join our activities. The efforts of our group have as their main aim that of reconstructing the lifestyle, culture and military equipment of the Thracian tribes in the period 400 BC–AD 100. With the passage of time, we also started to reconstruct other peoples living in the Balkans during Antiquity: Celts (300 BC–AD 100), Germani (AD 100–200) and Goths (AD 300–400). We try in our activities/reconstructions to be as historically accurate as we can. Our equipment is based on countless hours of interpreting ancient documents and archeological evidence; our process of research and experimentation never stops. During recent years we have participated successfully in several festivals in Bulgaria and abroad; we have also collaborated in the creation of various movies and books. All these positive experiences have increased our enjoyment and stimulated the general improvement of our group. Since we created 'Ancient Thrace', we have visited amazing destinations and met some great people, learned more about history and shared brilliant memories together. For us, historical re-enactment is a special passion that combines our interest with history with our desire to learn more about the past. We wish to reach people and share with them the emotions of this passion, which has become a very important component of our daily life.

Contacts:
Facebook: https://www.facebook.com/AncientThrace/

Historia Renascita

'Historia Renascita' is a re-enactment association from Romania, which approaches three different periods of Romanian history with its historical reconstructions: the era of the Dacian civilization from the reign of Burebista until the end of the Daco-Roman Wars (200 BC–AD 200), with special attention on the conquest of Decebalus'

Dacian Kingdom by the Romans of Emperor Trajan in AD 106; the period of the *Kievan Rus* (Middle Ages); and the period of the Great War. Regarding the ancient period, 'Historia Renascita' reconstructs Dacian warriors and civilians, Roman legionaries (of the *Legio IV Flavia Felix*) and other peoples from '*Barbaricum*' with which the Dacians came into contact (Celts, Sarmatians and Germani). 'Historia Renascita' has gained much experience in reconstructing the daily life of ancient peoples, participating during the last five years in more than seventy important festivals in Romania and other European countries. Our approach to historical re-enactment is a professional one, based on a rich documentation that is made up of historical and archaeological sources. We also create our activities/reconstructions with the help of specialists and researchers, whose competences are centred on the history of ancient Dacia. Our activities of experimental archaeology try to be as accurate as possible, and are all based on the material discoveries or written accounts provided by ancient historians (including Strabo, Dio Cassius, Trogus Pompeius, Iordanes, Plutarch, Ovid and many others). Obviously we also analyze the iconography of important ancient monuments, such as Trajan's Column, the Tropaeum Traiani, the Dacian statues from the former Forum of Trajan (some of which adorned Constantine's Arch of Triumph in Rome) and several others. We also consult all the latest academic studies and essays published on the history of ancient Dacia. The main objective of 'Historia Renascita' is to provide a significant contribution to the divulging of history, by trying to present all aspects in a balanced and objective way. The photographs reproduced in this book reconstruct accurately all the main typologies of Dacian warriors, and were realized with the help of photographers from the Alpha Studio of Pitesti in Romania, whom we thank for their precious support.

Contacts:
Email: historia.renascita@gmail.com
Facebook: https://www.facebook.com/historiarenascita/

Index

Abdera, 34, 43
Acamas, 4
Aenos, 34
Andriscus, 67
Antigonus Gonatas, 52
Antigonus Monophtalmus, 51, 53, 117
Antoninus Pius, 106
Aous, 63
Apollonia Pontike, 34
Archelaus, 58
Archialos, 34
Ariarathes, 55, 58
Artaxerxes, 40
Assuwa, 5–6, 8, 11–12, 14
Attalus III, 55
Aurelian, 106

Ballomar, 108
Bithyni, 14
Byzantium, 34
Byzone, 34

Callinicus, 70
Carians, 9
Cassander, 51
Cassius Dio, 91
Chaeronea, 45
Commodus, 110
Constantine the Great, 106, 174
Corinth, 67, 131
Corupedium, 52
Cunaxa, 40
Cynoscephalae, 63, 69
Cyrus the Great, 22, 24, 27
Cyrus the Younger, 40

Decius, 106
Delphi, 52, 81
Diurpaneus, 87

Domitian, 85, 154
Duras, 83, 85

Eumenes I, 55
Euphemus, 4

Gaius Porcius Cato, 81
Gallienus, 106

Halizones, 9
Hannibal, 61, 63
Hattusas, 5, 14
Herodotus, 15, 30
Homer, 1

Iliad, 1, 4, 6, 12
Ipsus, 51
Ismara, 12
Istros, 34

Kotys, 42–3, 114

Lake Trasimene, 61
Lycians, 9
Lysimachia, 34, 51–2

Maeonians, 9
Magnesia, 70
Maximinus I, 106
Messembria, 34
Muwatalli II, 6
Mysians, 9, 14

Nicomedes, 53, 55

Odessos, 34
Odyssey, 12
Oppius Sabinus, 85, 90

Pangaion, 45
Paphlagonians, 9
Peirous, 4
Pelasgians, 9
Perdiccas, 55
Philetaerus, 55
Pompey, 81
Prut River, 103
Ptolemy Keraunos, 52, 58, 117, 128
Ptolemy I, 51–2
Pydna, 67, 70
Pyrrhus, 51–2

Rhesus, 4, 12

Scorilo, 83
Siret River, 103

Tectosages, 58
Thyni, 14
Tolistobogii, 58
Tomoi, 34
Trocmi, 58
Tylis, 58

Wilusa, 6

Xenophon, 40

Zama, 63